THE RAPTURE
EXPOSED

THE RAPTURE EXPOSED

*The Message of Hope in
the Book of Revelation*

BARBARA R. ROSSING

A Member of the Perseus Books Group

Copyright © 2004 by Westview Press

Published in the United States of America by Westview Press, A Member of the Perseus Books Group, 5500 Central Avenue, Boulder, Colorado 80301–2877, and in the United Kingdom by Westview Press, 12 Hid's Copse Road, Cumnor Hill, Oxford OX2 9JJ.

Find us on the world wide web at www.westviewpress.com

Westview Press books are available at special discounts for bulk purchases in the United States by corporations, institutions, and other organizations. For more information, please contact the Special Markets Department at the Perseus Books Group, 11 Cambridge Center, Cambridge, MA 02142, or call (617) 252–5298, (800) 255–1514 or email special.markets@perseusbooks.com.

Library of Congress Cataloging-in-Publication Data
Rossing, Barbara R.
    The rapture exposed : the message of hope in the book of Revelation / Barbara R. Rossing
        p.   cm.
    Includes bibliographical references and index.
    ISBN 0–8133–9156–3
    1. Rapture (Christian eschatology)   2. Second Advent—Biblical teaching.
3. Bible. N. T. Revelation—Criticism, interpretation, etc.   I. Title.
BT887.R68   2004
236'.9—dc22

                                                          2003027965

Scripture quotations are from the New Revised Standard Version Bible, copyright © 1989, by the Division of Christian Education of the National Council of Churches of Christ in the United States of America.

The paper used in this publication meets the requirements of the American National Standard for Permanence of Paper for Printed Library Materials Z39.48–1984.

Typeface used in this text: 12-point Dante MT

10   9   8

To Ann E. Hafften—friend, writer,
Middle East advocate, peacemaker;

To Lauren Johnson, beloved husband

CONTENTS

PREFACE

In the years to come, many Americans will say that the terrors of September 11, 2001, changed their world. And many have turned to the Bible to seek answers and explanations for the reality of terror and evil. Publicly, the president turned to the Bible, and to hymns, using the image of God's "wonder-working power" to describe power of American people united to fight "evil-doers."

But what is the Bible's understanding of terror and evil? Or of God acting in the world today? Many answers can be found in the wonder-filled book of Revelation, but the answers will vary greatly depending on biblical interpretation and on which story you read.

One popular version of the story of Revelation captivated millions of Americans between the years 1995 and 2004. This story is not a Stephen King thriller or a Jackie Collins romance. It is a "Christian" novel series about the end of the world: the story of airline pilot Rayford Steele, whose wife was "Raptured" up to heaven while he was was flying a Boeing-747. It's about Steele's smart-as-a-whip daughter Chloe and journalist Buck Williams, who find faith and true love before they get busy thwarting evil for seven years of cosmic tribulation.

This is the story of *Left Behind*—twelve novels packed with conspiracy, romance, violence, and Bible verses. The high-tech adventures of born-again Christians give new life to the ancient biblical story of good versus evil. The villain they face is the Antichrist himself, the real one!

Reminiscent of Hal Lindsey's best-selling *The Late Great Planet Earth*—another end-times phenomenon that swept the country in the 1970s—these novels by Tim LaHaye and Jerry Jenkins have been teaching people to view world events in light of a very specific and violent biblical script. More than 50 million copies have sold; kids' books have been created, as well as a board game, a Web site, two movies, and numerous spin-offs—an enormous and lucrative end-times industry.

The notion of a violent biblical script or storyline for the end of the world is not unique to Hal Lindsey or the *Left Behind* novels. Whether on cable TV or radio, or in mega-churches across the country, fundamentalist preachers and televangelists are teaching their followers to correlate everything from failed United Nations peace plans, to earthquakes, to the September 11 terrorist attacks, with God's grand storyline. Floods, wars, heat waves, SARS, or other deadly diseases? Now it all makes sense as part of God's playbook, a cosmic countdown of ever-intensifying disasters leading up to what they view as God's "main event"—the final, bloody battle of Armageddon.

Fundamentalist Christian novels such as *Left Behind* "get a lot of people thinking about God who might not have otherwise," as my local librarian tells me. The books are fun and intense. They are easy to read. Like C. S. Lewis's *Space Trilogy*, the books create a fictional universe, giving readers ways to see themselves in relation to God through the characters' perspectives. That is the power of Christian fiction.

The trouble is, the interpretation of the Bible on which these books are based is also fiction. Today's end-times writings draw on a method for looking at prophecy that was invented less than two hundred years ago and, by now, is a dominant American view. In this system, the Bible—particularly the books of Daniel and Revelation—spell out in detail God's pre-ordained script of predictions for the end of the world.

Many other Christians read the biblical story differently, and I am one of them. The Bible does not provide a predictive screenplay for worldwide violence and disaster in the Middle East. Revelation's gift to us is a story of God who loves us and comes to live with us. Biblical prophets are not predictors of end-times events, they are inspired voices calling people to repentance and justice. They tell the wonderful and crucial story of God's faithfulness. They give us hope.

This book makes the case for that story.

This book is written for people young and old who are puzzled about the biblical book of Revelation and its end-times consequences for today. This book is written for those who have questions about the simplistic biblical script of "us" versus "them" promoted by the whole prophecy industry of Tim LaHaye, Hal Lindsey, and others. "My neighbor says that war in Iraq is part of God's plan in the Bible," a member of my church tells me. "What do I say when he starts quoting Bible verses he heard on TV about Babylon and Armageddon?" A student confides her fears to her pastor: "My friends say I'll get left behind when Jesus comes if I don't believe in the Rapture. They say I have to change churches or I won't be saved. I'm scared." In Jerusalem the questions are especially urgent: "Does Revelation really say that Israel must take over all the land and rebuild the temple on the site of the Dome of the Rock?" This is a question asked by both Jews and Christians working for peace. "Where do people get that belief, and how do we respond to it?"

What is at stake here is our reading of the Bible. Prophecy novels and televangelists offer people one particular storyline for our world, one reading of Revelation. I seek to offer a very different reading.

I believe that God is active in our world, but not in the ways that end-times enthusiasts envision. The book of Revelation is a crucial text for helping us see God's life in our world. For that reason we must reclaim this text from fundamentalists.

Revelation takes us on a journey—a journey not to war in the Middle East, but a journey into the heart of God, a journey into the heart of our world. Revelation's way of seeing teaches us how to look at the stories of our lives and the structures of violence and power in light of God's shepherding Lamb. It teaches us to challenge oppression and to look for signs of hope, even when evil seems overpowering. It gives us an urgent vision for our future in which God dwells with us, on earth. This is a vision that can guide us in a post-September 11 world.

A river of life flows through the Bible and the book of Revelation, a river flowing from the throne of God to bring healing to our world. Revelation offers its wondrous water of life as a gift to all who are thirsty for God's presence. This book is written to help people see and follow that biblical river in their lives.

The Destructive Racket of Rapture

If I knew the world were going to end tomorrow I would plant a tree.

MARTIN LUTHER

I need a new car. Something tells me it's going to be our only chance to survive.

"BUCK" WILLIAMS (TIM LAHAYE AND
JERRY JENKINS, *NICOLAE*, 12)

We need a shelter . . . I'm talking about getting an earthmover in here and digging out a place we can escape to.

REV. BRUCE BARNES
(LAHAYE AND JENKINS, *TRIBULATION FORCE*, 32)

THE RAPTURE IS A RACKET. Whether prescribing a violent script for Israel or survivalism in the United States, this theology distorts God's vision for the world. In place of healing, the Rapture proclaims escape. In place of Jesus' blessing of peacemakers, the Rapture voyeuristically glorifies violence and war. In place of

1

Revelation's vision of the Lamb's vulnerable self-giving love, the Rapture celebrates the lion-like wrath of the Lamb. This theology is not biblical. We are not Raptured off the earth, nor is God. No, God has come to live in the world through Jesus. God created the world, God loves the world, and God will never leave the world behind!

Rapture theology is disastrous for the Middle East and it is even more dangerous for planet earth. Proponents love to use the image of a countdown, reminiscent of a missile launch or space travel. God has a clock that is counting down, its hands drawing ever closer to midnight. Never mind that clocks and stopwatches were not invented until long after the Bible was written, it is their favorite image. God's prophetic stopwatch is ticking down to the end of the world.

John Hagee, pastor of the 15,000-member Cornerstone Church in San Antonio, borrows his particular doomsday clock from the *Bulletin of the Atomic Scientists*, an effort on the part of nuclear scientists to alert the world to the danger of nuclear annihilation. In 1947, these scientists initially set the hands of the clock at seven minutes to midnight. They periodically moved the hands closer or further from midnight depending on their evaluation of the global nuclear arms risk.

"God has a similar clock, my friend, and its hands *never* move backward," writes Hagee in the introduction to his book *Daniel to Doomsday: The Countdown Has Begun*. "Doomsday—the stroke of midnight—is coming." But note the crucial difference between Hagee's prophetic doomsday clock and that of the scientists. The nuclear scientists developed their clock to alert the world to our perilous situation *so that the hands will never reach midnight*. The scientists are trying to keep us from destroying the world.

Not Hagee. For him and other Rapture proponents the stroke of midnight on the doomsday clock is inevitable and even welcome. God plans to destroy the earth and there is nothing we can do to stop it. The countdown to the end is already under way. Each chapter of Hagee's book advances the clock one minute closer to midnight, culminating in the final chapter, entitled "Midnight: Doomsday at the Great White Throne," when the world comes to an end.

The Rapture is the reason Hagee and so many others revel in the prospect of destruction for the earth; the Rapture will be their "great escape" from earth. As Hagee boasts about the Rapture, *"Believers in Christ will escape doomsday!* Mark it down, take it to heart, and comfort one another with these words. Doomsday is coming for the earth, for nations, and for individuals, but those who have trusted in Jesus will not be present on earth to witness the dire time of tribulation."[1]

Similarly, Hal Lindsey writes, "Although I grieve over the lost world that is headed toward catastrophe, the hope of the Rapture keeps me from despair in the midst of ever-worsening world conditions."[2] He and other proponents of the Rapture are confident that Jesus will come to snatch or "Rapture" them up to heaven before unleashing a seven-year period of global tribulation and terrible destruction on the earth. Lindsey interprets Revelation's reference to "those who dwell in heaven" in chapter 12 of Revelation as proof that he and other Christians will not be found on earth during the woes and tribulation but rather will be part of "another special group called 'those who dwell in heaven.'"[3] Only non-Christians will suffer the fate of being "left behind" on earth.

In the summer of 2003 Ted Turner and Public Broadcasting System sponsored an eight-hour special "Avoiding Armageddon," warning of nuclear and chemical weapons proliferation and urging the world's leaders to take steps to curb the danger. The next week, in reviewing the week's news through her end-times lenses, a breathless Rexella Van Impe asked her husband on their fundamentalist Christian cable television show, "Jack, Ted Turner thinks Armageddon can be avoided. Is he right?" No, Armageddon cannot be avoided, was Jack Van Impe's enthusiastic reply to viewers. Van

Impe is the author of *The Great Escape: Preparing for the Rapture, the Next Event on God's Prophetic Clock* and other books on the Rapture and the Middle East. Like Hagee and Lindsey, he is confident that God will destroy the earth and also that he and Rexella will be raptured up to heaven before it all happens.

Rapture and Armageddon scenarios tap into Americans' love for disaster films and survivalist plot lines. Readers of end-times novels readily envision themselves among the select few who will escape planetary disaster. Like the remnant who survive an attack on the planet by alien creatures in the 1996 film *Independence Day*, or the couple who survey the devastation of New York City after the tidal wave caused by the impact from a comet in the movie *Deep Impact*, or survivors in the 1998 thriller *Armageddon*, readers of these scripts place themselves in the role of the elite individual heroes who will survive Armageddon or other disasters while the rest of the planet perishes. Even once-jailed televangelist Jim Bakker has now disavowed his previous pre-Tribulation Rapture theology as escapist, calling it a racket that preached a false gospel of prosperity—combined with the promise of escape from any consequences.[4]

Christ will return, on that the Rapture proponents and I agree. I pray for it each time I pray "Thy kingdom come" in the Lord's Prayer—a prayer that is never once prayed in the twelve *Left Behind* novels. Jesus taught an urgency about his kingdom in this prayer that is still very much alive for Christians today.

But we completely disagree on what that urgency means for the world and for our life today. We differ, first of all, on our views of God—whether our God is a God whose will is to destroy the world. Second, we differ on whether Christians are to embrace an escapist ethics, as Rapture proponents argue, or are to urgently love and care for the world in anticipation of Christ's return, as I advocate. These differences in ethics will be crucial for our future.

GOD STILL LOVES THE WORLD—
GOD DOES NOT DESTROY THE EARTH

Jesus is coming back at a moment we cannot know. But that does not mean that God is getting ready to destroy the earth and take Christians away to another planet. A Presbyterian pastor taught me a Rapture song he learned as a child: "Somewhere in outer space God has prepared a place for all those who trust him and obey . . . The countdown's getting closer every day." This song reflects a key point on which the Rapture teaching is false and dangerous. There is *no place* in outer space to which God will take us to escape the earth. This is not the biblical message. We cannot trash this planet and assume there is another.

Space imagery is frequent in Hal Lindsey's *Late Great Planet Earth*. Published in 1970, just one year after astronaut Neil Armstrong walked on the moon, Lindsey's book appealed to people's desire for the adventure of space travel in describing the Rapture as the "ultimate" space trip.

> Astounding as man's trip to the moon is, there is another trip which many men, women, and children will take someday which will leave the rest of the world gasping . . . Without benefit of science, space suits, or interplanetary rockets, there will be those who will be transported into a glorious place more beautiful, more awesome, than we can possibly comprehend . . . It will be the living end. The ultimate trip. (Hal Lindsey, *The Late Great Planet Earth* [Grand Rapids, Mich.: Zondervan, 1970], 135–137)

Left Behind author Tim LaHaye also engages in planetary speculation regarding earth's destruction and the creation of the "new earth" of Revelation 21. He explains how God's future timetable "does away with this planet as we know it" in two events of destruction.[5] Earth's first destruction will be by fire while the second destruction will be more severe, and will include even the atmosphere. Here LaHaye fabricates a distinction between three different heavens in the Bible—the atmospheric heaven around the earth, which he says is the "abode of Satan"; a second, stellar heaven that contains the stars; and the third heaven, the heaven of the throne of God in the visions of Revelation 4 and 5, which will not be destroyed. The atmospheric heaven is what God plans to destroy in Revelation 21:1, according to LaHaye. "God will destroy this earth that is so marred and cursed by Satan's evil. He will include the atmospheric heaven to guarantee that all semblance of evil has been cleared away."

Only after those two destructions will God create a new heaven and a new earth, says LaHaye. He fantasizes that the new earth may not be "limited to the twenty-five thousand miles in circumference and eight thousand miles in diameter of the present earth. It may be much larger; the Bible does not say." In addition to a larger-size earth, LaHaye speculates about how the new planet won't waste any space with oceans or mountains or deserts, since such landscapes are uninhabitable for humans and are therefore "worthless."

This kind of speculation would be amusing if it were not so dangerous. God created the earth's mountains and deserts and called them "good"—they are not worthless to their Creator. Earth's atmosphere, too, was created by God, and God laments over it when we destroy it. The atmosphere is under assault today from ozone depletion, increasing concentrations of carbon dioxide that cause global warming, and other wounds—but these are wounds caused by humans. The atmosphere is not the abode of Satan. The view that total planetary and atmospheric destruction must take place on earth before God's renewing vision of "New Jerusalem" can come into the world is not biblical. It leads to appalling ethics.

To be sure, Revelation proclaims a "new heaven and a new earth," but that does not mean that God gives us a replacement for this current earth when we damage it beyond recovery. A new earth is not something we go out and get as born-again hero Buck Williams gets a new car in the *Left Behind* novels. Rather the earth becomes "new" in the sense of resurrection or renewal—just as our bodies will be resurrected, brought to new life, but they are still our bodies. The whole creation is longing for redemption, the apostle Paul writes—this is the sense in which there will be a new creation. It, too, will be redeemed, made new.[6] The Greek word used for the "new" earth in Revelation 21:1 can mean either "renewed" or "new"—but it certainly does not mean a "different" earth. There is no justification for using up the earth on the grounds that we get to trade this one in for a new and bigger one in seven years.

Reagan-era Secretary of the Interior James Watt told U. S. senators that we are living at the brink of the end-times and implied that this justifies clearcutting the nation's forests and other unsustainable environmental policies. When he was asked about preserving the environment for future generations, Watt told his Senate confirmation hearing, "I do not know how many future generations we can count on before the Lord returns." Watt's "use it or lose it" view of the world's resources is a perspective shared by many Rapture proponents, whose chief preoccupation is counting down to earth's violent end.

Even more extreme is a recent remark by right-wing pundit Anne Coulter: "God gave us the earth. We have dominion over the plants, the animals, the trees. God said, 'Earth is yours. Take it. Rape it. It's yours.'"[7]

Raping the earth and justifying such behavior on the grounds that this earth is ours and it will be finished in seven years is like saying we might as well use drugs and abuse our bodies because we know we will soon be resurrected with new bodies. Our bodies are God's temple, the apostle Paul tells us in his letter to the Romans. They are not to be abused but rather reverenced. God dwells in these earthen vessels. Similarly with the body of the earth: It, too, is a body God created and still calls good. It is a temple in which God dwells. We do not leave this earth behind. God does not leave it behind and neither can we.

The British author C. S. Lewis's *Chronicles Of Narnia*, a popular series of Christian novels from the mid-twentieth century, depicts salvation in a much more earth-affirming way than the *Left Behind* story. When Lucy and her companions finally come into the "New Narnia" at the end of their journey in Lewis's *The Last Battle*, it is not an escape from their homeland but rather a going through a door more deeply *into* God's picture, into the world. The travelers slowly come to realize that the place is the very same place as the world they left behind: the same hills as those in their hometown, the same house, but everything is more radiant. The color blue is bluer. It is "more like the real thing." New Narnia is different from old Narnia in being a "deeper country: every rock and flower and blade of grass looked as if it meant more."

New Narnia is "world within world," Lucy realizes. The Faun Tumnus explains the within-ness of God's vision for our world: "You are now looking at the England *within* England, the real England." Most importantly, in Lewis's vision—contrary to the destructive Rapture script—"no good thing is destroyed."[8] This is the wondrous land Lucy and her companions have been looking for all of their lives. A donkey named Puzzle, a Mouse, an Owl, the Good Badger, and "all the dear creatures" go with them into the new landscape.

The Narnia story's ending gives a much truer reading of the final vision of the book of Revelation than the *Left Behind* story. The Narnia story is also more faithful to the biblical covenant with Noah. The book of Genesis tells how, after the flood, God made a covenant with Noah never again to destroy the earth: "I will never again curse the ground because of humankind . . . nor will I ever again destroy every living creature as I have done."[9] Does Revelation now negate that covenant with Noah, as Rapture enthusiasts suggest? Has God's mind changed? Would God now destroy the earth? Some argue that the promise to Noah was only that God would not use a *flood* the next time in destroying the earth, but that fire or nuclear war might not be a violation of God's covenant. References to a fiery end in the Second Epistle of Peter are favorite texts for those who make this argument. But the biblical promise to Noah is "never again." There is no indication that God will suspend the promise of caring for the earth for what Lindsey, Hagee, and LaHaye claim will be seven years of end-times tribulation. The Bible is clear: God so loved the world, and God continues to love it. Sadly, what gets "left behind" by the Rapture plotline is the Bible itself.

Even in the Genesis flood, God took care to save animals of every species—a signal of God's love for the whole created world. But today's Rapture proponents have no such love for creation. Their Rapture saves only humans. Animals and plants get left behind on earth to suffer destruction. Writes Lindsey, "As the battle of Armageddon reaches its awful climax and it appears that all life will be destroyed on earth—in this very moment Jesus Christ will return and save man from self-extinction." Note that only "man" is saved from extinction in this script—none of the other species that God also created to fill the earth with magnificent biodiversity survive. Birds, butterflies, flowers, trees, badgers, and "all the dear creatures," as C. S. Lewis calls them in the *Chronicles Of*

Narnia —these have no place in the fundamentalists' plan for the future. It is an astonishingly narrow and self-centered view.

The nineteenth-century former slave Sojourner Truth criticized the escapism and self-centeredness in the Rapture rhetoric among Christians of her day. In response to claims that Christians are taken up to some parlor in heaven to escape destruction, she underscored that God stays with us on earth and walks with us through every trial:

> You seem to be expecting to go to some parlor *away up* somewhere, and when the wicked have been burnt, you are coming back to walk in triumph over their ashes—this is to be your New Jerusalem!! Now I can't see anything so very nice in that, coming back to such a muss as that will be, a world covered with the ashes of the wicked. Besides, if the Lord comes and burns—as you say he will—I am not going away; I am going to stay here and stand the fire, like Shadrach, Meshach, and Abednego! And Jesus will walk with me through the fire, and keep me from harm. (Quoted in Lee Griffith, *War on Terrorism and the Terror of God* [Grand Rapids, Mich.: Eerdmans, 2002], 193)

Jesus walks with us through the fire. That is the message of the book of Revelation, as Sojourner Truth articulated.[10] God's people experience trials and tribulation. The message of the Bible is that God comes to dwell with us and walk with us through all the events of our lives.

The Bible's message is not that "God so loved the world that he sent World War III." God will judge evil—Revelation is clear about that. But God is not a God who will destroy the earth, either by fire or by nuclear war. Nor does God approve of our destruction of the earth. God laments over any harm done to the earth by us or by anyone else, crying out with a cosmic cry of "Alas for the earth."

GOD'S DWELLING WITH US VS.
LEFT BEHIND'S "MANICHEISM"

Whatever future events await the earth, the biblical message is that God comes down to earth to live on it with us. Earthquakes, darkness, plagues? God comes. Are hearts breaking? Is all hope lost? God comes. At one of the bleakest moments in history, when people of Judea and Galilee groaned under Roman occupation some two thousand years ago, "the word became flesh and dwelt among us," John's Gospel tells us. God came to be born in the world. Jesus is God's final word incarnate in the world and that word is "yes."[11] God loves the world enough to live in it.

If we want to find God today we must also stoop low—to look into the manger in which Jesus was born, to find God in the small things, in the daily stuff of earth. God is not to be found in the violent Red Horse of the Apocalypse but incarnate in the holiness of everyday life. As poet Gerard Manley Hopkins writes so eloquently, "The world is charged with the grandeur of God." His poem is an evocative invitation to see God's presence everywhere in the world around us. "Nature is never spent; There lives the dearest freshness deep down things. . . Because the Holy Ghost over the bent World broods with warm breast and with ah! Bright wings."[12]

God does not come to take us away from this earth, but rather comes to dwell with us in every joy and every sorrow, in every blazing display of nature's beauty that is never spent. That God's spirit is still brooding over our world with "ah! Bright wings" points us here, to the earth, to the events of daily life, to find God's presence in the world.

This important message seems to be missing from Rapture theology. Where are God and Jesus to be found today? The *Left Behind* novels seem to suggest that God is largely removed from the earth, inflicting plagues and earthquakes on it ("The Wrath of the Lamb

Earthquake") but otherwise living up in heaven, waiting for the end of time. Jesus will make one quick foray back to swoop up the church in the Rapture, but even then he will only hover above the earth. In their view, Jesus will not touch down again on earth until seven years after the Rapture, when he comes to set up his kingdom in the Glorious Appearing.

Such "Beam me up" theology risks falling into a new form of Manicheism—the centuries-old heretical belief that the world is evil and that our goal is to escape. Manicheism, a form of Gnosticism, was a dualistic heresy that divided the world into absolute good and evil. To refute this dualistic heresy, the early church stressed the bodily incarnation of Christ in the flesh and the goodness of creation.

Manicheistic tendencies surface repeatedly in the *Left Behind* novels, in comments such as Buck's observation that going outside the safe house in Chicago means going out into "a hostile world that belonged to the Antichrist and the False Prophet," and especially in repeated references to the Antichrist as "the ruler of this world." [13] The Bible would never allow the claim that the world "belongs" to the Antichrist! According to Revelation 1:5, Jesus—not Antichrist—is the "ruler of the kings of the earth." When Jesus said in the Gospel of John that "the ruler of this world is cast out" he confirmed that evil powers once ruled the world—but that they were cast out once and for all. Satan no longer rules. In Christ's death and resurrection "The kingdom of this world *has become* the kingdom of our Lord and of his Christ" (Rev 11:15). God's rule is not reserved for the future. Revelation's message to Christians today is the same as to its original first-century readers: that Jesus—not Antichrist, nor Caesar, nor any president or imperial leader—is the true ruler of the world.

To be sure, God's presence in our world is often difficult to see. We live in an in-between time—the time between the "already" of

Jesus' life, death and resurrection and the "not yet" of his Second Coming. Christians must hold both of these facts in tension, even when they seem contradictory. Until Christ comes again, in the Second Coming, the kingdom of God is not yet fully present. But we must guard against Manicheistic tendencies that imply that God has left the world behind.

NEW INDIVIDUALISTIC ETHICS FOR THE END-TIMES

The world cannot be saved—that is the basic Rapture credo, proclaimed by televangelists, radio preachers, and best-selling end-times thrillers. Rapture proponents seem willing to live in the world with no more responsibility for caring for it than just letting the clock run out. They love to cite statistics about how the world is getting worse: crime is on the increase, wars and earthquakes are more frequent, the oceans are polluted, environmental degradation is worsening. To them, these "signs" prove that the prophetic clock has counted down almost all the way and then they can soon escape.

Until Christ's return, Rapture proponents focus on saving individuals out of the world. Their goal is to tell as many people as possible about Christ before it is too late. Historian Paul Boyer notes that this is the basic stance of premillennialist Christians. "Mankind's collective doom was certain, but *individuals* could escape."[14] In reaction against the "social gospel" movement of the early part of the twentieth century, Rapture theology emphasized that the goal is "not to make the world better," but to "save people out of" the world.[15] Chicago evangelist Dwight L. Moody used the image of a shipwreck—"individual survivors might be rescued, but the vessel itself was beyond hope."[16] Historian Randall Balmer calls it a theology of despair.[17]

Moreover, in the *Left Behind* view of the end-times, normal life gets suspended as the countdown gets closer. Hero Buck Williams was probably a law-abiding driver in normal circumstances. But the *Left Behind* message is that times are no longer normal. In these final days on the cusp of a new era or "dispensation" in God's prophetic clock, the rules are suspended and ethics shift. Every male reader's road-rage fantasy is fulfilled when Buck bypasses a long line of traffic: "Buck had never had patience for traffic jams . . . His jaw tightened and his neck stiffened as his palms squeezed the wheel . . . Inching along in near gridlock made the huge automotive power plant feel like a stallion that wanted to run free." Buck's "stallion" gets the chance to run free when an explosion rocks Chicago:

> Buck saw a mushroom cloud slowly rise and assumed it was in the neighborhood of O'Hare International Airport . . . Buck looked quickly behind him and out both side windows. As soon as the car ahead gave him room, he whipped the wheel left and punched the accelerator. Chloe gasped as the car jumped the curb and went down through a culvert and up the other side. Buck drove on a parkway and passed long lines of creeping vehicles.
>
> "What are you doing, Buck?" Chloe said, bracing herself on the dashboard.
>
> "I don't know what I'm doing babe, but I know one thing I'm not doing: I'm not poking along in a traffic jam while the world goes to hell." (Tim LaHaye and Jerry Jenkins, *Nicolae: The Rise of Antichrist*, vol. 3 of *Left Behind* series [Wheaton, Ill.: Tyndale House Publishers, 1998], 9–10)

Buck's decision to bypass the long line of cars makes perfect sense in the *Left Behind* mentality that the end-times are upon us and only born-again individuals matter. So does his decision to drive right to the car dealership and buy the largest, most powerful car he can possibly afford—a fully loaded Range Rover "under six figures." After all, gas mileage and global warming are hardly a concern if the planet only needs to last seven more years.

Left Behind's fascination with violence also escalates in the later novels. Just about every Tribulation Force member carries an Uzi or a Directed Energy Weapon (DEW), although Chloe's gun is just an "ancient Luger."[18] A believer who lives in Greece articulates *Left Behind*'s theology of guns and prayer: "There is nothing wrong with working while someone is praying. Someone put extra ammunition clips in a bag while I pray. Our God, we thank you . . ."[19] This is not normal life. But ammunition clips and prayer give a fair representation of *Left Behind* preparations for the end-times—getting us ready for the final show-down when Christians will battle the Antichrist and his forces.

Their justification for focusing on such violent and drastic scenarios is that we are already living at the brink of the end-times. Although their new final "dispensation" in history with its new rules will not officially start until after the Rapture and Antichrist's signing of a seven-year treaty with Israel, every Rapture writer or televangelist today gives the impression that the end-times have in some sense already begun. Hagee explicitly argues that the end-times began on September 11, 2001. "We are seeing in my judgment the birthpangs that will be called in the future the beginning of the end," he told a BBC interviewer. "I believe in my mind that the Third World War has begun. I believe it began on 9/11."

Hal Lindsey uses the image of a fuse that was lit with Israel's rebirth in 1948. History is now racing toward the end, like a lighted fuse. The pace is accelerating.

Jesus is coming. We can agree on this. Christians are to live every moment as if the world may end tomorrow. But the crucial question on which we differ is this: How do Christians live if you know you are living in the end-times? That is a question writings such as the *Left Behind* novels address in a way very different from the classic Christian response. They answer in terms of bunkers, Range Rovers, high-security satellite phones, and computers to out-smart the Antichrist. The unraptured pastor in *Left Behind* comes up with the idea of building an underground bunker in which the members of his Tribulation Force can hide out and evangelize over the Internet. Each member is equipped with a computer, satellite phone, and encryption technology more powerful than the Antichrist's. As Buck specifies, "Money is no object . . . I want a computer with virtually no limitations. I want to be able to . . . connect with anyone anywhere without the transmission being traced . . . I want all of it, Donny, and I want it fast."[20]

Contrast this bunker mentality to the traditional Christian understanding in Martin Luther's oft-quoted remark that "If I knew the world were going to end tomorrow I would plant a tree." Luther is saying he would continue to live even more deeply rooted in the confidence of God's love for the world. "Thy kingdom come *on earth* as in heaven," is what Jesus taught us to pray. It is not a prayer to take us away from earth, nor a prayer for escape in a bunker, but a prayer that God's reign will come to earth—and that it will even come "through us," as Luther explains.

Fortunately the New Testament itself deals with that very question of how to live if you know the world is going to end—indeed, that is the central question in the book of Revelation and in other New Testament writings. Early Christians definitely thought they were living at the brink of the end-times. The Apostle Paul taught in First Thessalonians that most of them would still be alive for Christ's return. So how did they live? Did they go out and buy things, to use them up? Did they clear-cut the forests? Did they suspend the rules? Did they become an underground high-tech Tribulation Force with a mission to conquer evil through violence, stealth, and better fire power?

No, they cared for one another and for their neighbors in a very public and open way. Love of neighbor and hospitality to strangers was Christians' surest response to life on the brink of the end times. They gathered together and worshiped God, convinced that "Jesus has set up here on earth a community that is an alternative to empire," as Chilean scholar Pablo Richard describes early Christian ethics in his powerful commentary on Revelation.[21] Early Christians ministered to the poor. They visited prisoners. They broke bread together, they sang hymns to God and the Lamb. As a second-century opponent of Christianity, Governor Pliny, described Christians' conduct in a letter to the emperor Trajan, early Christians would "pledge themselves by an oath not to engage in any crime, but to abstain from all thievery, assault and adultery, not to break their word once they had given it, and not to refuse to pay their legal debts."[22]

The early Christians nurtured community. The Greek word *koinonia* or "communion" was a core commitment for them, and by that they meant not a tight little band of like-minded "Tribulation Force" comrades as in *Left Behind*, but an all-embracing and joyous fellowship as citizens of God's new community, open to the world. Revelation calls their lifestyle "patient endurance" or "resistance" (the Greek word *hypomene*, first used in Rev 1:9 and throughout the book). By their patient and subversive lifestyle of love and welcome and community, the early Christians resisted the claims of empire. They lived in light of the vision of the Lamb that had changed their lives. And people around them marveled at their joy and boldness.

Early Christians did not fight. They engaged in spiritual warfare only by using the weapons of love—loving their enemies and praying for those who persecuted them. Seeing this amazing self-giving love—not displays of Christians' superior technology or miraculous powers—was what persuaded many pagans to convert to christianity. Martyrdom was also a powerful testimony.

The *Left Behind* novels completely reverse the early Christian understanding of how to live in the end-times. Rayford, Buck, Chloe, and the other characters spend most of their time tracking or evading the Antichrist on their sophisticated computers and bugging devices, and working to get their message out on the Internet. Only a minimal amount of time is devoted to above-ground hospitality or love of neighbor beyond their little tribe. The message that "God so loves the *world*" is nowhere to be found.

Translating the *Left Behind* novels' ethics into life for us today leads to the inevitable conclusion is that we, too, can suspend normal ethical imperatives because of the end-times. That means suspending concern for things like the environment or violence. Violence becomes more attractive if you don't have to worry about the long-term consequences of weapons' proliferating or community stability. Wasteful and polluting choices are fine if you do not care about healing the world, if you are not concerned for the health of your grandchildren and future generations. The Rapture vision invites a selfish non-concern for the world. It turns salvation into a personal 401(k) plan that saves only yourself.

With this book I will make the case for a different interpretation of Revelation and indeed, for a different version of Christianity. One goal will be to reclaim "traditional" Christian interpretations of Revelation in the face of the recent and problematic invention of the Rapture. I will counter Rapture theologians' misinterpretation of prophecy as a predictive script for the future and challenge the politics of their escapist end-times storyline. Additionally, I will seek to offer a more earth-affirming reading that can speak to urgent issues that we face today.

The Invention of the Rapture

TEN-YEAR-OLD "JOSH" CAME HOME from school to an empty house. His mother, normally at home to greet him, was nowhere to be found. She might have been at the store or at a neighbor's, but Josh was terrified. His immediate response was a terrible fear that all his family had been "Raptured" without him. Josh was sure he had been left behind.

Now a grown-up in my seminary class on the book of Revelation, Josh told this story of his boyhood experience. Others consistently echo his story of childhood fear of the Rapture. These born-again Christian children were exhorted to be good so that they would be sure to be snatched up to heaven with Jesus when he returned. Raised on a daily diet of fear, their view of God resembled the song about Santa Claus coming to town: "You'd better watch out, you'd better not cry." Only it was Jesus, not Santa, who was "coming to town" at an unexpected hour: "He knows when you've been sleeping. He knows when you're awake. He knows if you've been bad or good, so be good for goodness sake."

Christian camp songs taught children to count down to the Rapture like a space launch:

Ten and nine, eight and seven, six and five and four;
Call upon the Savior while you may.
Three and two, coming through the clouds in bright array.
The countdown's getting closer every day.

The Presbyterian pastor who shared this song with me experienced an unexpected and disturbing flashback to his childhood fears even as he sang the words. Visibly shaken after one of my talks on the Rapture, he was experiencing real panic: "I thought I was over the Rapture trauma, but I guess I'm not."

All this fervor and fear over the Rapture—a principle invented only 170 years ago—for a word that cannot even be found in the Bible.

The countdown image perfectly expresses the theology of the Rapture and the end-times. Christian end-times movies have been marketed as thrillers. *A Thief in the Night*, from 1972, is described as "the most popular end-times movie ever produced, with over 300,000,000 viewers." The heroine "disregards prophetic biblical warnings and the truth begins to unfold. Can she escape the dramatic, haunting circumstances? Is there a way out? The climax is riveting!"

Cloud Ten Pictures' trilogy, *Apocalypse, Revelation,* and *Tribulation,* employed real Hollywood stars Gary Busey, Margot Kidder, and Corbin Bernsen. And most recently the movie version of *Left Behind* (2000), by LaHaye and Jerry Jenkins, created a huge buzz in the Christian media, but was roundly scorned by mainstream reviewers.

In every depiction the Rapture divides families. Terrified parents on airplanes scream, "My babies, my babies," as the camera cuts to teddy bears and diapers left behind on the seats. All children under age twelve disappear. Babies are sucked out of pregnant women's wombs as stupefied fathers watch the ultrasound machines go blank. Planes and cars crash in fireballs. Media reports come in from around the country: "Trains were involved in head-ons with lots of death."[1] God had Raptured the engineers before they had time to apply the brakes.

Does the Bible really teach that Jesus will come to snatch Christians off the earth, causing "lots of death," before inaugurating a seven-year period of tribulation? The Rapture has become embedded in American Christian culture today, but the idea of the Rapture is less than two hundred years old.

No specific passage in the Bible uses the word "Rapture." Even today's most famous Rapture proponents, LaHaye and Lindsey, admit that. Nor does the Bible clearly lay out their version of God's prophetic timetable. Details "must be pieced together from various passages of Scripture," explains LaHaye in his 2002 book *The Rapture: Who Will Face the Tribulation?* LaHaye is the theological brains behind the *Left Behind* novels, the plots of which are written by Jenkins. LaHaye has written numerous books about the end-times and is a long-time leader in right-wing Christian political causes along with his wife, Beverly.

Most Christian churches and biblical scholars condemn Rapture theology as a distortion of Christian faith with little biblical basis. Critics represent the whole spectrum of churches, from conservative Missouri Synod Lutherans to evangelicals, to Roman Catholics, and liberal Presbyterians. Many evangelical churches and leaders oppose the notion of the Rapture, pointing out that it is a recent and idiosyncratic development in Christian teaching. But institutional criticism is essentially irrelevant. It is through popular televangelists and writings such as Lindsey's *The Late Great Planet*

Earth and the more recent *Left Behind* novels that the Rapture storyline has become central to so many Americans' understanding of the Bible and Christian faith.

✶ DARBY'S RAPTURE

The Rapture has its origins in the nineteenth century—beginning, according to one critic, with a young girl's vision.[2] In 1830, in Port Glasgow, Scotland, fifteen-year-old Margaret MacDonald attended a healing service. There, she was said to have seen a vision of a two-stage return of Jesus Christ.[3] The story of her vision was adopted and amplified by John Nelson Darby, a British evangelical preacher and founder of the Plymouth Brethren.

At the time, the belief that Jesus will come again was not new. Christians have always taught that Jesus will return to earth and that believers should live in the urgent and hopeful anticipation of his second coming. This teaching is central to ancient Christian creeds and is taught by all churches. But Darby's new teaching was the claim that Christ would return *twice*. The first return would be in secret, to "Rapture" his church out of the world and up to heaven. Christ would return a second time after seven years of global tribulation to establish a Jerusalem-based kingdom on earth (which they call the "Glorious Appearing," a phrase from Titus 2:13). For Darby and his sympathizers, the search was on for Bible verses to support this two-stage version of Christ's return.

Although the word "Rapture" does not occur in the Bible, believers explain that it comes from the Latin word *raptio*, a translation of the original Greek for the word "caught up" as it is used in Paul's First Epistle to the Thessalonians: "Then we who are alive, who are left, will be caught up together with them to meet the Lord in the air; and so we will be with the Lord forever" (1 Thess 4:17).

Darby made a number of mission trips to America between 1859 and 1877 and won many converts to the Rapture idea. Unlike other end-times enthusiasts, such as Seventh Day Adventist founder William Miller who had specified dates for the end of the world in the 1840s, Darby refrained from predicting a specific date for Christ's return.

Instead, he invented "dispensations"—that is, intervals of time ordering God's grand timetable for world events. From this expression came "dispensationalism," a particular system or school of thinking about the end-times reflecting Darby's premise. According to Darby's view, God has divided all of human history into seven distinct dispensations, or ages, and during each time God has dealt with people according to a different set of rules. Dispensationalism thus lays out a rigid master plan for all of history.

An important tool for popularizing Darby's system was the *Scofield Reference Bible*, a best-selling work published in 1909. It has been called "perhaps the most important single document in all fundamentalist literature." Cyrus I. Scofield was a dubious character who embezzled money, served six months in jail for forgery even after his conversion to Christianity, and abandoned his wife and daughters, according to critics.[4] Scofield hit the jackpot with his annotated *Scofield Reference Bible*, a version of the King James Bible in which he added dispensationalist headings and notes in the margin commenting on each prophetic passage in light of Darby's system. With sales in the millions, it became the version of the Bible through which Americans read their scriptures throughout much of the twentieth century. Scofield's notes and headings were woven in with the biblical text itself, elevating dispensationalism to a level of biblical authority that no previous writing had.

Prophecy conferences and radio programs sponsored by Chicago's Moody Bible Institute and a number of Bible schools elabo-

rated on Darby's timetable and end-times system. Early dispensationalist promoters included wealthy Chicago businessman
William Blackstone (author of the 1878 work *Jesus is Coming*), an
avid Zionist, and Lewis Chafer, a Presbyterian who founded the
dispensationalists' training center, the Dallas Theological Seminary, in 1924. More recent disciples of Darby include the many
graduates and associates of Dallas Theological Seminary such as
John Walvoord (president of the seminary from 1952 to 1986),
Charles Ryrie, and Hal Lindsey, as well as televangelists, Bible
school graduates, and many others.

"I praise God for a man like John Darby," writes Lindsey, whose
best-selling *The Late Great Planet Earth* updated Darby's system
with Cold War politics and nuclear weapons in the 1970s. Lindsey
continues to revise his views to accommodate shifting world politics, with Islam now replacing the old Soviet Union as the
Antichrist *du jour* in his most recent dispensationalist timetables.
LaHaye's many writings over the past thirty years also follow
Darby's system.

People are attracted to Darby's dispensationalist system with its
Rapture theology because it is so comprehensive and *rational*—
almost science-like—a feature that made it especially appealing
during battles over evolution during the 1920s and 1930s. With the
ascendancy of Darwin and sweeping scientific claims in the nineteenth century, many people responded to a biblical "system" that
could compete with science in its rationality and approach to history. Proponents admit that the dispensationalist system is not
spelled out in any single passage in the Bible. Nevertheless they
insist that a comprehensive system is necessary and that Darby's
dispensationalism, with its divisions of history and its two-stage
future return of Christ, is "the only system" that can make sense of
otherwise contradictory biblical passages.

Without this principle of distinct ages of human history, times when God deals with the world differently, they argue, "the Bible cannot be understood as a consistent and cohesive whole. The only other alternative is to allegorize large portions of scripture . . . in order to keep the Bible from contradicting itself."[5] When the goal is to put scripture on the level of science there can be no loose ends, no allegory, and certainly no contradictions.

CONSTRUCTING DANIEL'S PROPHETIC COUNTDOWN

To understand the biblical basis for much of today's end-times thinking we have to begin our story further back than the book of Revelation. In the view of Darby and other dispensationalists, God's whole biblical plan for the end-times is already mapped out in the Old Testament. The entire end-times framework of Darby's dispensationalist system is based on just three verses at the end of chapter 9 of Daniel!

Daniel 9:25–27 gives a chronology of seventy "weeks" of Israel's history—with a day representing a year in this apocalyptic book. How to interpret this opaque passage from Daniel is the great question that divides dispensationalists from most mainline Christians. The three verses from Daniel describe 490 years of Israel's history as follows:

> From the time that the word went out to restore and rebuild Jerusalem until the time of an anointed prince, there shall be seven weeks; and for sixty-two weeks it shall be built again with streets and moat, but in a troubled time. After the sixty-two weeks, an anointed one shall be cut off and shall have nothing, and the troops of the prince who is to come shall destroy the city and the sanctuary. Its end shall come with a flood, and to the end there shall be

war. Desolations are decreed. He shall make a strong covenant with many for one week, and for half of the week he shall make sacrifice and offering cease; and in their place shall be an abomination that desolates, until the decreed end is poured out upon the desolator. (Dan 9:25–27; New Revised Standard Version)

In the view of most scholars, the desolation and abomination that Daniel described in the final verse happened long ago, when the tyrannical emperor Antiochus Epiphanes desecrated the Jewish temple and set up a statue of the Greek god Zeus in 168 B.C. (see also Dan 11:31). Daniel was using apocalyptic imagery to challenge the political oppression that people were suffering in his own time.

But for Darby and proponents of his system, Daniel's final seventieth week with the desecration of the Jewish temple has not yet happened. It remains "unfulfilled prophecy," awaiting fulfillment in some not-too-distant future time. According to Darby and the dispensationalists, the first 483 years of the Daniel prophecy were fulfilled in ancient Israel's history only up through week number sixty-nine.

But something happened! With the crucifixion of Jesus Christ, "God obviously stopped 'the prophetic stopwatch'" one week short of the end. "The clock could not have continued ticking consecutively," asserts Lindsey, since Rome's destruction of the Jerusalem temple in 70 A.D. did not follow the chronology of Daniel in the literalist way dispensationalists require.[6]

God paused the prophetic stopwatch for two thousand years because the Jews, who should have crowned Jesus as their Messiah and king, rejected him. God was forced to stop the clock and turn to a different plan, starting yet another dispensation of human history. With language like "God was forced," dispensationalists put God in a corner in a way that traditional theology would never permit—but a sense of prophetic inevitability is necessary for their system.

According to dispensationalists, Israel's prophetic stopwatch has been stopped now for the past two thousand years. We are currently living in a "parenthesis" or "gap" on the divine stopwatch, between Daniel's sixty-ninth and seventieth weeks. This is an astounding claim, based on three obscure verses in Daniel. All of church history is just a "time-out"—what dispensationalists call the "church dispensation" or church age, or "God's great parenthesis in history." Any minute now, God will remove true Christian believers from the earth in the Rapture, keeping the church completely separate from Israel—a key element in the system —and then the prophetic stopwatch can resume for the final "week" or seven years of Israel's history. It's all prophesied in Daniel 9:27, they say.[7]

This interpretation of Daniel is challenged by most mainline Christians, including Catholics, Lutherans, Methodists, Presbyterians, and most evangelicals. Critics point out that if you actually read these verses in Daniel, there is no indication of a gap of thousands of years before the final seventh "week" of years. The gap is imported into the text because Rapture enthusiasts need it to make their prophetic framework fit with Israel's history. Such a move strains their claims of literalism, however, since there is no "plain sense" warrant for inserting a chronological gap into the Greek or Hebrew texts.[8]

GOD OF THE GAPS

Dispensationalists are masters at importing such "gaps" into biblical prophecy. Often the gaps are necessary because they view that all references to Jesus' kingship as "unfulfilled prophecy," to be fulfilled only after Jesus wins the battle of Armageddon and literally sits down on David's throne in Jerusalem. Their view that Jesus is not yet a king causes dispensationalists to arbitrarily split up Bible verses with gaps of thousands of years.

For example, San Antonio-based pastor and author John Hagee claims that the first part of the familiar prophecy of Isaiah 9:6—"For unto us a child is born, Unto us a Son is given"—was fulfilled in Jesus' birth. But the second part was not fulfilled, he says, the part that says "the government shall be upon his shoulders, and his name shall be called 'Wonderful, Counselor.' The second part will only be fulfilled thousands of years after Jesus' birth, in Jesus' future millennial kingdom. So a single verse from Isaiah 9:6 actually refers to "two widely separated events in history."[9] Needless to say, most scholars view the insertion of thousand-year gaps into Isaiah or Daniel as a complete fabrication on the part of dispensationalists.

Other gaps arise from dispensationalists' insistence on an almost apartheid-like separation between Israel and the church. The separation of the "church dispensation" from "Israel's dispensation" was one of Darby's key tenets. Dispensationalists are to be commended for challenging the idea that the church somehow supercedes Israel. Yet their notion of the church as an entity completely separate from Israel contradicts the New Testament conviction that the Gentiles are also co-heirs to God's promises to Israel. There is no biblical basis for dispensationalist claims that the church has to be "Raptured" off the world stage before God can deal separately again with Israel.

Other gaps are necessitated by dispensationalists' insistence that every detail of a biblical verse must be literally fulfilled in history. Unless this criterion is met they assign verses to their category of "unfulfilled prophecy"—even when the Bible itself states that a prophecy has already been fulfilled! In Acts 2, for example, the apostle Peter clearly states that the birth of the church at Pentecost fulfilled the Old Testament prophet Joel's prophecy of "these last days":

> This is what was spoken through the prophet Joel: "In the last days it will be, God declares, that I will pour out my Spirit upon all flesh, and your sons and your daughters shall prophesy ... And I will show portents in the heaven above and signs on the earth below, blood, and fire, and smoky mist. The sun shall be turned to darkness and the moon to blood, before the coming of the Lord's great and glorious day. Then everyone who calls on the name of the Lord shall be saved." (Acts 2:16–21)

But LaHaye denies that Joel 2 was "fully" fulfilled on Pentecost, contrary to the apostle Peter himself, since the sun was not literally turned to darkness nor the moon literally turned to blood. LaHaye has the audacity to argue that "What Joel said next *did not happen on that Pentecost*, so long ago ... This whole passage in Joel awaits consummation at the end of the Tribulation."[10] LaHaye's assertion is a direct contradiction to Peter's words of scripture in Acts 2. Such rigid literalism violates even the Bible itself.

The greatest problem with the dispensationalist system, however, is simply Darby's premise that three verses of Daniel provide what proponents view as "God's whole chronological framework for the future." Neither Jesus nor any of his New Testament followers understood the book of Daniel as encompassing this kind of overarching plan for history, nor do Jews. Jews do not even consider Daniel among the prophetic books. Probably because of its late date, the Jewish Bible assigns Daniel among the "Writings," not the Prophets.

Dispensationalists claim that God has ordained a prophetic plan for all of world history and "nowhere is God's prophetic plan more fully illustrated than in the book of Daniel."[11] But there is no New Testament basis for constructing such a master plan for history, much less for basing their plan on three verses in Daniel. Even in the book of Acts, when the apostles Peter and Paul cite the Old

Testament to preach about Jesus in terms of God's history in the world and Old Testament prophecy, they never turn to the book of Daniel.

The dispensationalist system is a fabrication of Darby—as Lutheran historian Martin Marty warns, a system "invented less than 200 years ago in the British Isles, shipped to America, exported to the world," that must be challenged today both because of its false theology and also because of its growing influence on public policy.[12]

RAPTURE OR RESURRECTION?
JESUS' RETURN IN THE NEW TESTAMENT

Once Darby formulated the overall framework of dispensationalism and the Rapture around Daniel 9, all other prophetic Scripture passages had to be interpreted to fit this timetable. "Charting the End Times" became an obsession.[13] As Lindsey describes his detailed charts elaborating on Daniel 9:27, "Using this framework, I'm going to fit the many other prophecies together." So in the New Testament, Jesus' promise of the "many mansions"[14] in his Father's house in John 14 became "the first teaching about the Rapture in the Bible," according to LaHaye.[15]

Another favorite New Testament text is Titus 2:13: "Waiting for the blessed hope and the glorious appearing of the glory of our great God and savior, Jesus Christ," in the King James Version. According to Rapture proponents, this verse from Titus describes two distinct events, separated by a seven-year "gap" or interval. The "blessed hope" refers to the Rapture, while the "Glorious Appearing" will happen seven years later, after the tribulation. Of course, there is no indication in Titus 2:13 itself that the "glorious appearing" describes a different event from the "blessed hope"— most biblical scholars think the two phrases refer to the same thing and that there is no seven-year gap between them. But that is not a problem for those who come to this verse with a predisposed view of the Rapture already well in place.

The majority of New Testament passages on which dispensationalists base the notion of Rapture concern either resurrection or Jesus' second coming—neither of which is the same as the Rapture, despite dispensationalists' claims.

Resurrection is the foundational event for Christian faith. Ancient Christian creeds proclaim that God raised Jesus from the dead and declare that "We believe in the resurrection of the dead," a belief shared by all Christian traditions today. But this is certainly not the same as saying that believers will be "Raptured" up from the earth to heaven.

A favorite proof-text for Rapture proponents is First Corinthians chapter 15. In *Left Behind*, a pastor had the foresight to record a video in advance for people who would be left behind. "Let me show you from the Bible exactly what has happened," the fictional pastor tells unraptured viewers. "As this tape was made beforehand and I am confident that I will be gone, ask yourself, how did he know? Here's how, from 1 Corinthians 15:51–57."[16] The pastor then reads to his video audience from St. Paul's first letter to the Corinthians:

> Behold, I tell you a mystery: We shall not all sleep, but we shall all be changed—in a moment, in the twinkling of an eye, at the last trumpet. For the trumpet will sound, and the dead will be raised. (1 Cor 15:51)

The pastor proceeds to interpret this verse from First Corinthians 15 as if it were describing Rapture—based on Paul's words "changed" and "raised."

But take a closer look at this verse from First Corinthians and you see that what St. Paul was writing about is not Rapture but the resurrection from the dead—as can be seen from the phrase "the dead will be raised." Apparently some Christians in first-century Corinth did not believe in resurrection from the dead and Paul wrote to them to correct their theology—"How can some of you say there is no resurrection of the dead?" Paul challenges the Corinthians. Even though Paul uses the term "raised from the dead" and clearly states that his subject is resurrection, dispensationalists nonetheless use 1 Corinthians 15 to argue for the Rapture: "When these things have happened, when the Christians who have already died and those that are still living receive their immortal bodies, the Rapture of the church will have taken place," the fictional video argues.[17]

In his nonfiction books, Left Behind author LaHaye makes explicit his interpretation of Rapture as equivalent to resurrection. "Christ is coming to resurrect and translate His church. We call that the Rapture."[18] Call it what you want, such wholesale appropriation of resurrection texts for Rapture—including Jesus' teaching that "I am the resurrection and the life" and Jesus' raising of Lazarus in the 11th chapter of John's Gospel—raises questions about the strength of LaHaye's Rapture argument. Rapture is not the same as resurrection in Christian theology. Even First Thessalonians 4, another favorite proof-text for the Rapture, proclaims resurrection, not Rapture, when Christ returns again to earth (see Epilogue).[19]

Other biblical passages used by enthusiasts to argue for Rapture concern Jesus' second coming. Like resurrection, the belief that Christ will return to earth again is foundational for Christians—but this is not the same as the Rapture. All ancient creeds declare that Jesus "will come again to judge the living and the dead and his kingdom will have no end." But nowhere do the creeds or the Bible describe Jesus as returning twice, or in "two distinct stages" separated by a period of seven years, as dispensationalists claim. The

New Testament describes Jesus' second coming in a great variety of ways, sometimes focusing on heaven, sometimes on earth; some verses focusing on judgment and others on salvation; some depicting a banquet with the Old Testament prophets or a marriage feast, others a paradise or garden or fields of green pastures, and others a wonderful city with golden streets. The promises are rich and varied, more lavish than we can possibly imagine.

Fortunately, God does not call upon us to systematize the promises into one humanly constructed timetable or make them all fit into a system "like a completed puzzle."[20] Dispensationalists like to divide promises about Jesus' second coming into two distinct lists, arguing that "irreconcilable differences exist between them" unless you distinguish promises about heaven (the "Rapture") from promises about earth (the "Glorious Appearing").[21] They seem to think God wants us to figure out the chronology like puzzle pieces. But God's promises are not lists or puzzle pieces set forth for us to figure out. To arbitrarily separate the Bible's descriptions of Jesus' return into two lists, assigning one list to the "Rapture" and the other to Christ's "Glorious Appearing" scheduled for seven years later, is not biblical. The New Testament is rich in its descriptions, but it knows of only *one* second coming of Christ, not two.

RAPTURE IN REVELATION?

In their search to find the Rapture in many other New Testament books, LaHaye and Lindsey argue that the Rapture is also taught in Revelation 3:10, where Jesus tells the church in Philadelphia: "I will save you from out of the hour of trial." Most scholars think the "hour of trial" refers to a political trial or even the possibility of persecution for Christians at the time when Revelation was written. LaHaye, however, emphasizes the Greek preposition "out of" and argues that this means Christians will have been snatched out of the earth before the seven-year tribulation begins, although the word in the text is "trial," not "tribulation."

Moreover, Lindsey and LaHaye claim they can point to the moment in Revelation when this escape from the earth happens: Revelation 4:1, when the author, John, is told to "Come up here" to heaven. This verse is the last time the word "church" is mentioned in the book—therefore the church must have been Raptured up to heaven with John as of Revelation 4:1, they say.

In this scenario, believers will watch from a safe distance in heaven as God unleashes the plagues of Revelation's seals, trumpets, and bowls upon the earth for seven years. The church will then return to earth with Christ and his armies, after the tribulation is all over, for the battle of Armageddon and the thousand-year reign.

But such an escapist interpretation is the very opposite of the message of Revelation, as we shall see. While the word "church" is not used after Revelation 4, "the saints" are very much present on earth during Revelation's judgments, and they are the same group of people as the church. In Revelation 18:4 the church is directly addressed as "my people"—a big problem for dispensationalists who think the church is absent during these chapters.

No, the message of Revelation is that God hears the cries of the church, the cries of "my people," and of oppressed people everywhere on earth. Life for God's people on earth involves tribulation, sometimes severe. John, the author of Revelation, writes not to urge escape from suffering or tribulation but to emphasize that he already "shares in tribulation" with his churches (Rev 1:9). The meaning of the word "tribulation" can be very broad in the New Testament. The apostle Paul uses the same word, "tribulation" (in Greek, *thlipsis*), to describe the sufferings he endured, including imprisonment, persecution, beatings, and physical illness. Whatever the tribulation, Paul and other early Christians would surely be shocked to hear dispensationalists' interpretation that the church will escape tribulation by being Raptured out of the world.

Tribulation is not just a future event, according to Revelation. John shares in tribulation with people like "Antipas," a martyr in the city of Pergamon, named in chapter 2, who remained faithful to death despite tribulation. John shares in tribulation with people through the centuries who have endured unspeakable suffering and tribulation, and have found in Revelation's songs and visions a sense of hope. From the townships of South Africa to villages in El Salvador where whole populations were "disappeared," God's people continue to turn to Revelation's liberating visions for comfort and solidarity in tribulation. We insult such saints and their brave witness if we say that tribulation is only in the future end-times and that Christians will be Raptured up off the earth before it begins.

Christians are not dealt a get-out-of-tribulation-free card to play in the face of the world's suffering and trials. Such escapism underscores one of the biggest problems with dispensationalist theology. Jesus never asked of God to "Beam me up" from the earth, nor can we. It is a temptation we must resist—as Jesus did. Tribulation is something that has happened and is still happening today for many of God's people in the world. God saves us not by snatching us out of the world, but by *coming into the world to be with us*. This is the central message of Jesus' incarnation and of the Bible. It is the central message of the culminating chapters of Revelation, the New Jerusalem vision of chapters 21–22. God still loves the world. The Bible proclaims an incarnational faith—God coming to earth—not Christians escaping from earth via the Rapture.

Some Rapture proponents deal with this charge of escapism by delaying the Rapture until midway or all the way through the supposed seven-year tribulation. These are called "mid-Tribulation Rapture premillennialists" and "post-Tribulation Rapture premillennialists." LaHaye rebuts them in point-by-point arguments, as does Lindsey. Through their rebuttals, however, Lindsey and LaHaye are forced to concede the tenuous nature of all Rapture arguments because of the lack of Bible verses: "The truth of the matter is that neither a post-, mid-, or pre-Tribulationist can point to any single verse that clearly says the Rapture will occur before, in the middle of, or after the Tribulation," Lindsey acknowledges.[22] To Lindsey's statement we can only say "Amen." The reason he is unable to point to a single biblical verse clarifying the Rapture chronology is that the Rapture itself is an invented idea. Fabricated by Darby, the notion of any kind of Rapture—whether pre-Trib, post-Trib, or mid-Trib—was imported into the Bible only 170 years ago.

SEVEN YEARS OF TRIBULATION?

Their future seven-year period of tribulation after the Rapture is another example of dispensationalists' chronology that has no scriptural basis. This timetable is criticized not only by biblical scholars but also by church leaders such as Illinois's Roman Catholic bishops who voice the concern that church members and others "have internalized this fictional post-Rapture time of tribulation when sinners are left to battle the Antichrist, because it sounds familiar and 'biblical.'"[23]

Television preachers like Jerry Falwell, Pat Robertson, Jack Van Impe, and others preach the seven years of post-Rapture tribulation so constantly that many Americans assume it must be in the Bible. LaHaye claims that "the Bible devotes more space to the seven-year Tribulation than it does to any other historical period"—a startling claim if he means that the Tribulation eclipses Jesus' life and teachings as portrayed in the gospels![24]

But contrary to the charts and timelines that are so popular with dispensationalists, Revelation makes no references to "seven years."

While Revelation frequently uses the number seven, and Revelation also refers to "tribulation"—primarily to describe hardships that first-century Christians were already suffering or would soon face—Revelation never mentions a future seven-year period of tribulation. Like the Rapture, the timetable of a seven-year period of tribulation is a recent development that dates back only to Darby's nineteenth-century system. While the seven years of tribulation may "sound familiar and biblical," as the Catholic bishops warn, in fact they are not biblical.

Proponents claim that the seven-year timeframe of tribulation comes from that same crucial verse in the Old Testament book of Daniel, Daniel 9:27: "He shall make a strong covenant with many for one week," with a week being understood in Daniel not as seven *days* but as seven *years*.[25] Proponents then argue that chapters 6 through 19 of Revelation give us the detailed chronology of events scheduled to happen during that period of Daniel's seventieth week of years. In addition to Daniel 9:27, LaHaye and others also claim to find their seven years by combining the forty-two-month span of Revelation 11:2 ("Do not measure the court outside the temple . . . it is given over to the nations, and they will trample over the holy city for forty-two months") with the 1,260-day period of Revelation 11:3, to add up to an approximate total of seven years.

But if chapter 11 of Revelation supposedly spells out the seven years of tribulation, it is striking that not one of the three crucial words—"seven," "years," or "tribulation"—is found in Revelation 11. Why did Revelation not make the seven-year calendar more explicit, if Daniel's "seven years" provides the chronological framework for the book? With Revelation's propensity for sevens—seven numbered seals, trumpets, and bowls—Revelation should highlight this sequence of seven years, if it is key to the book's timetable. Only by rewriting Revelation for their own purposes can dispensationalists claim to find seven years of tribulation in this book.

While dispensationalists' seven-year tribulation rests on a highly questionable biblical basis, it nonetheless makes for an action-packed storyline. All the *Left Behind* novels are set within Revelation's supposed seven years of tribulation after the Rapture, updated with the latest in high-tech weaponry, satellite phones, and computers. The novels are based on a questionable theological premise, criticized even by many conservative evangelicals, that during the seven years of tribulation un-Raptured people who are left behind on earth will be given a second chance to convert to Christianity. Conservatives argue that the Bible never gives any hope of a second chance after Christ's return. But the second-chance premise is necessary for the heroic adventures of *Left Behind*'s "Tribulation Force" over the course of seven years—and twelve novels.

FICTIONALIZING REVELATION

LaHaye says he first got the idea for the novels when he was on an airplane flight and noticed the pilot flirting with the flight attendant. The pilot "had on a wedding ring and she didn't. I thought what if the Rapture were to occur now and the pilot was left behind, but his wife wasn't. That was the first seed of my idea."[26] That seed grew into a twelve-novel series, the "all-time best-selling Christian fiction series," according to the Left Behind Web site, beginning with the vignette of a fictional airline pilot, Rayford Steele, flirting with the flight attendant. Hundreds of passengers are suddenly reported missing, including all the children on the plane. All over the world, people have vanished without a trace. Driverless cars crash in huge pile-ups. Rayford makes his way home through the rubble to find his wife's nightgown and wedding ring on the pillow. Rayford realizes the Rapture had happened and he was left behind. He and other non-Raptured Christians must band together to form the elite Tribulation Force that will win people for Christ and oppose the evil Antichrist during the next seven years.

Death and destruction flow forth from every one of the *Left Behind* novels, from frequent references to World War III and the "Wrath of the Lamb Earthquake" to the final battle of Armageddon. As each of Revelation's seals is opened, as each trumpet is blown, the violence escalates and the tribulation intensifies. Millions of people are killed in these and other end-times novels—not by bows and arrows, as in the biblical scenes, but by assault rifles and missiles fired from helicopter gunships. New weapons are the most striking way that Lindsey and LaHaye "update" Revelation to sell their books today.

In his 1970s best-selling *The Late Great Planet Earth*, Lindsey pioneered the technique of "translating" Revelation's tribulations into twentieth-century weaponry. Lindsey claimed that the author of Revelation actually foresaw modern nuclear warfare and weaponry in great detail. Here's how: In Revelation's description of *"something like* a great mountain burning with fire" that is thrown into the sea (Rev 8:8–9), Lindsey explains, John is "giving an accurate description of a thermonuclear naval battle in terms of his first century experience." Lindsey uses time-travel to explain how John gained such knowledge of weaponry centuries ahead of his time:

> John heard and saw things that would happen on earth some nineteen hundred years later. How in the world would a first century man describe the highly advanced scientific marvels of warfare at the end of the twentieth century? . . . John was hurtled by God's Spirit through time up to the end of the twentieth century, shown the actual cataclysmic events of the Tribulation, then returned to the first century and told to write about what he had witnessed. (Lindsey, *The Rapture: Truth or Consequences*, 101–102)

Throughout the 1980s and 1990s, Lindsey continued to "update" John's visions of weaponry and geopolitics with revised editions of his book. To keep the prophecies of Revelation current with ever-new global threats and political alliances, Lindsey quietly discarded previous prophecies and military scenarios that had gone out of date.

Updating of Revelation's violence into high-tech twenty-first-century weaponry gives Lindsey's and LaHaye's books an up-to- the-minute thriller appeal for contemporary audiences. "The authors can't be unaware that slaughter, theological or non-theological, sells books," observes Jana Reiss of *Publishers Weekly*. "No previous Christian novel has detailed so many revolting ways for innocent civilians to bite the dust." Indeed, before the *Left Behind* series concluded with the twelfth novel in 2004, Tyndale Publishing House had already launched a new military spin-off series, recapitulating the same storyline from the perspective of American military rangers stationed in the Middle East. Titled *Apocalypse Dawn*, the new series capitalizes on a popular feature of *Left Behind*—violence. Evil figures are not the only ones who carry guns and use them in these books. An ethos of righteous Christian violence permeates all dispensationalist rhetoric today, fiction and nonfiction alike. Hagee's latest Christian novel is called *Avenger of Blood*, while LaHaye's new *Babylon Rising* promises that is it a prophecy "thriller" even more fast-paced than the *Left Behind* novels.

All this violence and slaughter is necessary because it is predicted in the Bible, according to dispensationalists. Using flip charts the pastor who was not raptured in *Left Behind* lays out the supposed biblical schedule of future cataclysms and violence. "Rayford was furiously taking notes . . . How could he have missed this?" *Left Behind* asks.[27] Our answer, of course, must be that Rayford and millions of other Christians missed it because it was never in the Bible in the first place. A British preacher named Darby invented this point of view centuries after the Bible, and the *Left Behind* authors and other dispensationalists are using it to further their particular social and political agenda.

By this time we should ask what else dispensationalists put forward that might be hard to find in the Bible. When proponents assert that some event is biblical without citing the exact biblical verse, it is fair to suspect that no clear-cut biblical passage supports their claim. Gary DeMar, a conservative evangelical critic, lists in his *End Times Fiction: A Biblical Consideration of the Left Behind Theology* a number of unsupported assertions in the dispensationalist script, especially concerning the Middle East:

- There is no mention of a rebuilt Jerusalem temple anywhere in the New Testament, including Revelation;
- Neither Daniel nor Revelation uses the word Antichrist;
- There is no record in Revelation or Daniel of the Antichrist making a covenant with Israel;
- There is no record in Daniel or Revelation of the Antichrist breaking the covenant with Israel;[28]
- There is no mention that Jesus will set up an earthly throne in Jerusalem.[29]

Dispensationalists will argue that each of these so-called events rests on solid biblical evidence. Their arguments are convoluted and complex, relying on dubious "gaps" of thousands of years. To make sense, their biblical chronology must combine bits and pieces of the Bible written many centuries apart and under very different circumstances into one overarching narrative. Their chronology of a rebuilt temple in Jerusalem, for example, brings together the "Antichrist" from the epistle of First John with an isolated verse from Daniel and another verse from Revelation. Their seven-year tribulation chronology combines Revelation's sole reference to a "great tribulation" with Daniel 9's "seventieth week," along with Jesus' discourse in Matthew 24–25.

But surely this is not how John nor Matthew nor any other biblical writer intended their writings to be used, as bits and pieces to be cut and pasted into an end-times formula. The Bible is neither puzzle pieces to be fitted together nor isolated verses to be mined for their predictive code. "Ironically, in their effort to interpret the Bible literally and consistently, proponents of the Rapture have mangled the biblical witness almost beyond recognition," charges New Testament scholar Craig Hill. "It is the Bible itself, this wonderfully diverse and complex witness to God and Christ, that has been left behind."[30]

"GOD SO LOVED THE WORLD THAT HE SENT WORLD WAR III?"

RAPTURE, TRIBULATION, AND FOREIGN POLICY

As we have seen, the dispensationalist Rapture script distorts the Bible. But more than that its distortion is increasingly shaping American culture and political beliefs. Dispensationalists put forth a whole sequence of global political events that supposedly must follow after the Rapture during the tribulation, especially in Israel and the Middle East—and many Americans are eagerly waiting and counting down for these disastrous events to happen in our lifetime.

Increasing numbers of believers think that the dispensationalist timetable will literally happen on the world stage. They believe that an Antichrist figure will most certainly come to power and will manipulate the United Nations, just as Nicholas Carpathia does in the *Left Behind* novels or President Mark Beaulieu does in Pat Robertson's *The End of The Age*.[31] "I have opposed the United

Nations for fifty years," LaHaye boasts of his involvement in right-wing political causes. With his best-selling *Left Behind* novels, LaHaye has created a powerful platform for influencing mainstream America through his fictional characters' perspectives on a whole range of conservative political issues including anti-abortion, anti-homosexuality, anti-environmentalism, militarism, and Middle East policy, as well as opposition to the United Nations.

For Christians who buy into this dispensationalist theology, the only question is where we are today in the prophetic countdown and how to fit today's global political events into God's timetable. The Left Behind Prophecy Club's Web site, for example, encourages readers to make direct connections between its end-times script and contemporary politics: "Have events in Iraq launched an unstoppable chain that leads to Armageddon? Could the Antichrist be alive now? Is the UN a precursor of the One World government prophesized in the Bible? Are ATMs and other revolutions in banking foretelling of the Mark of the Beast? Is SARS a fulfillment of Jesus' prophecy about plagues in the End Times?"

Such speculations may sound more like a horoscope than serious politics. But consider that the political practice of correlating apocalyptic biblical verses with foreign affairs already made front-page news some twenty years ago, in the speculations of President Ronald Reagan. In a conversation with a lobbyist for the influential American Israel Public Affairs Committee, a pro-Israel group, Reagan wondered about biblical prophecy coming to fulfillment in the violent events of the Middle East: "You know, I turn back to your ancient prophets in the Old Testament and the signs foretelling Armageddon, and I find myself wondering if—if we're the generation that's going to see that come about. I don't know if you've noted any of those prophecies lately, but believe me, they certainly describe the times we're going through."[32]

President Reagan's remarks were widely criticized by politicians as well as by Christian and Jewish communities. Nancy Reagan reportedly groaned when her husband was asked again about the subject of Armageddon in the 1984 presidential debates.[33] Israeli Jewish theologian Yehezkel Landau wrote an editorial suggesting that the president's use of violent and absolutist biblical imagery in reference to the Middle East reflected a false view of prophecy. In Landau's view, the presidents of both the United States and Israel "ought to engage in some prophetic self-criticism in the exercise of political power" rather than invoking biblical apocalyptic imagery to support violence:

> The true prophetic spirit today would address these root conditions of injustice, instead of branding the Eastern bloc nations, or the Syrians, or the Iranians, as the "children of darkness" who will be vanquished at Armageddon by the virtuous defenders of the true faith executing God's wrath. (Yehezkel Landau, "The President and the Prophets," *The Jerusalem Post*, Nov. 1983, reprinted in *Christianity and Crisis* as "The President and the Bible," Dec. 12, 1983)

Such abuse of biblical prophecy, Landau ruefully concluded, "boils down to this perverse parody of John 3:16: 'God so loved the world that he sent it World War III.'"[34]

Armageddon and presidential apocalyptic rhetoric resurfaced again in foreign policy debates some twenty years later—in speeches promoting the "war on terrorism" and the Iraq War—with dangerous implications, in the eyes of much of the world. "We are in a conflict between good and evil. And America will call evil by its name," President Bush told West Point graduates in 2002, drawing on dualistic apocalyptic imagery.

In the months leading up to the 2003 Iraq War, historian Paul Boyer voiced concern about the "shadowy but vital way that belief in biblical prophecy is helping mold grass-roots attitudes toward current U.S. foreign policy." Boyer is a scholar of dispensationalism and its impact on U.S. politics, and is best known for his 1992 book, *When Time Shall Be No More: Prophecy Belief in Modern American Culture.* In that work he analyzed the role of prophecy belief during the Cold War, especially in the Reagan White House.

Boyer's 2003 article in *The Chronicle of Higher Education* pointed to the recent burgeoning of premillennial belief in the USA— "upwards of 40 percent" of Americans, according to 2002 polls— and its impact on foreign policy. In Boyer's view, the rhetoric of apocalypse popularized by the *Left Behind* novels and other dispensationalist texts helped to drive the U.S. march toward war in Iraq:

> When our born-again president describes the nations' foreign-policy objectives in theological terms as a global struggle against "evildoers" . . . he is not only playing upon our still-raw memories of 9/11. He is also invoking a powerful and ancient apocalyptic vocabulary that for millions of prophecy believers conveys a specific and thrilling message of an approaching end—not just of Saddam, but of human history as we know it. (Boyer, "When U.S. Foreign Policy Meets Biblical Prophecy," *The Chronicle of Higher Education*, Feb. 14, 2003)

The arguments of Boyer and others about the apocalyptic influence of the dispensationalist novels on U.S. policy were picked up by *Business Week* ("Bush, the Bible, and Iraq") and also by overseas publications ("Behold the Rapture," *The Economist*, August 2002; "Bush Puts God on his Side," BBC, April 6, 2003). Televangelist Van Impe boasted on air that he has been contacted by the Bush White House National Security Advisor's staff to give his view of current events in the Middle East in light of biblical prophecy. To be sure, his claim has not been substantiated. President George W. Bush has

not spelled out his own beliefs about dispensationist biblical interpretations regarding the Middle East, although some of his cabinet
members are more overt. But the widespread influence of such
prophecy beliefs may play a role in explaining America's apocalyptic rhetoric of war and evil—and possibly even actual policy deci-
sions coming out of the White House.

The influence of dispensationalism can be seen also in fundamentalist Christians' opposition to the U.S.-backed "Road Map" for
peace in Israel and Palestine. "The Bible is my Road Map," declares
an Internet petition circulated by Robertson, Falwell, and LaHaye
in opposition to a negotiated solution to the Israeli-Palestinian conflict. Peace and peace plans in the Middle East are a bad thing, in
the view of fundamentalist Christians, because they delay the
countdown to Christ's return. Israel must not compromise by giving back any occupied territory to the Palestinians. New Israeli settlements and a rebuilt third temple are God's will for Israel, no
matter how violent the consequences.

The dispensationalist version of the biblical storyline requires
tribulation and war in the Middle East, not peace plans. That is the
most terrifying aspect of this distorted theology. Such blessing of
violence is the very reason why we cannot afford to give in to the
dispensationalist version of the biblical storyline—because real
people's lives are at stake.

The Rapture Script for the Middle East

The veil between the fiction of Left Behind and the reality of life in the Middle East today is a thin one.

LEFT BEHIND WEB SITE

THE SINGLE PLACE WHERE A CHANGE is most urgently needed in the way Christians understand Revelation's message is in regard to the land of Israel and Palestine. Real people in the Middle East currently stand to lose if American Christians, following the dispensationalist script, succeed in shaping foreign policy according to their view of the Bible. With their warlike endtimes script, dispensationalists have supported an all-or-nothing mentality of conquest for Israel, and they look forward to more violence in Israel as the so-called prophetic countdown to the end approaches. Their militant, triumphalistic vision for the future of Jerusalem stands in sharp contrast to Revelation's vision for Jerusalem as a holy city for all peoples, with open gates and a wondrous tree of life—a place of welcome and healing.[1]

The dispensationalist movement is very public in the Middle East, particularly among foreign Christian groups visiting or living there. Revelation is its foundation—not Revelation's healing story of the nonviolent Lamb, but the story of the wrathful lion-like Jesus who will return to Israel to fight a battle in which blood will flow up to horses' bridles. The platform is a conservative social agenda led by a Middle East policy that aggressively supports the modern state of Israel's expansionism and blocks efforts for peace. This is the program of "Christian Zionism," a renewed and accelerating subset of fundamentalist Christianity.

This is not traditional Zionism, broadly defined as support for Israel as a secure Jewish homeland. My own Lutheran church and most mainline churches are on record as strongly supporting Israel in the classic sense of Zionism. But the new movement of "Christian Zionism" is a militant all-or-nothing kind of Zionism that scripts Israel as a player in the dispensationalist Christian end-times drama in a way that baffles even Israelis, although some are willing to accept its support. This all-or-nothing Christian Zionism, reflected in the writings and speeches of Lindsey, LaHaye, Hagee, and other dispensationalists, is simply "heresy," as Lutheran Palestinian bishop Munib Younan states.

In the American media, Christian Zionist spokespeople function as evangelists for Armageddon with a confident and sophisticated presence—on satellite TV networks and Web sites. Exhorting biblically based support for the state of Israel, they overlap and intertwine their roles as preachers, political commentators, political organizers and fund-raisers. It is a well-organized strategic campaign, combining all the components of a political campaign, a military campaign and gala media event. Supporters include televangelists Jack Van Impe, Benny Hinn, Jerry Falwell, Pat Robertson, much of Christian radio, and many others. The Christian Broadcasting Network and the Trinity Broadcasting Network regularly feature Christian Zionist programs. The International Christian

Embassy in Jerusalem and other organizations are think-tanks for the movement.

Ridiculous interpretations of the Bible—Revelation and the book of Daniel, in particular—drive this accelerating campaign forward. It is a complex and highly developed undertaking directed by a theology whose believers look toward escape from this world rather than life in a "peaceable kingdom" together with God on earth.

This view is distorted and dangerous. It is a hazard to peace—a militant script for the Middle East that ends with Armageddon.

THE FOUNDING OF ISRAEL IN 1948: A PROPHETIC SUPER-SIGN?

After dispensationalist thinking got started with the writing of Darby in the 1830s, it was not long before the political side of the movement also took off. Dispensationalists in both the United States and Great Britain were involved in the Zionist movement throughout the nineteenth and twentieth centuries, based on their convictions about biblical prophecy.

When the state of Israel was established in 1948, American fundamentalists sat up and took notice. Bible prophecy being fulfilled in their own time, the Bible coming to life! Statehood for Israel was the first of a number of specific things they believed had to come to pass before Jesus could return to earth. Preachers and believers met the news with a wave of enthusiasm and support.

This was *the* key event on God's prophetic end-times time clock, according to Lindsey, LaHaye, and many fundamentalists. That event was "the first in a chain of biblically mandated events that will culminate in the return of Jesus and the end of history," writes journalist Jeffrey Sheller.

Where is the founding of the modern state of Israel mandated in the Bible? In his 1970 best-selling *The Late Great Planet Earth,* Lindsey invented the now-popular interpretation of Jesus' fig tree parable in Matthew 24 as a text in which "Jesus predicts an extremely important time clue" about the date for his return. Matthew reads as follows:

> From the fig tree learn its lesson: as soon as its branch becomes tender and puts forth its leaves, you know that summer is near. So also, when you see all these things, you know that he is near, at the very gates. Truly I tell you, this generation will not pass away until all these things have taken place. (Matt 24:32–33)

Never mind that Jesus himself didn't identify the fig tree as Israel. Lindsey interpreted Israel as the fig tree; and "putting forth its leaves" was Israel becoming a sovereign state—the prophetic "super sign" signaling that Jesus was at the gates and could return any minute:

> The figure of speech "fig tree" has been a historic symbol of national Israel. When the Jewish people, after nearly 2000 years of exile, under relentless persecution, became a nation again on 14 May 1948 the "fig tree" put forth its first leaves. (Lindsey, *The Late Great Planet Earth*, 55)

Lindsey's interpretation of the fig tree as Israel has become commonplace among dispensationalists. Lindsey further explains that "this generation" in Jesus' parable of the fig tree means the generation that saw the founding of Israel. Therefore, "within forty years or so of 1948, all these things could take place," he wrote in 1970 about the return of Christ. Needless to say, Lindsey backed off from that statement as 1988 approached and it became clear that the Rapture and the end of the world were not happening within forty years of Israel's founding, contrary to his original prophesy. This is just one of the many changes Lindsey has quietly made in his prophetic script over the years as world events turned out differently from his predictions.

But is Israel's founding really necessary in order for Jesus to be able to return, as dispensationalists claim? If so, then we must ask about previous generations of Christians who lived before 1948. For thousands of years, faithful Christians living from earliest times through the modern day have watched and prayed for the return of Jesus without believing his coming was contingent on a new state of Israel. Were all these Christians misguided to think that Jesus could return in their own lifetimes?

According to this mentality, most New Testament Christians would have to be considered misguided as well. The New Testament contains many books written after the fall of Jerusalem in 70 A.D. whose authors knew full well that Jews no longer had a state of their own. Yet all of them preached about the imminent return of Jesus. Take the book of Revelation, written years after Rome reconquered Israel. Revelation expects Jesus' return any minute, but never does the book mention Israel's rebirth as a prerequisite to that return. No passage in the New Testament makes Jesus' return contingent on the re-establishment of a Jewish state.

There are more severe consequences to the dispensationalist Christian interpretation of scripture, and they fall upon the other community living in the same Holy Land. Palestinians in the West Bank, Gaza, and East Jerusalem—many who have been refugees with their families since 1948—feel the crushing weight of this triumphalistic understanding of biblical prophecies. Driven from their homes in Jaffa, Haifa, or the Galilee by fear or forced expulsion, they fled to shelter with relatives or into refugee camps. And there they stayed, hunkered down in poverty, awaiting some kind of international resolution that never came. Did biblical prophecy require that an angel or flaming sword drive them out so that present-day Israel could be born? No, of course not. That version of the apocalyptic script is a violent betrayal of Christian understanding.

In the latest scenario of what is required before Jesus can return, a Jewish state is not enough. Beyond their original references to the *founding* of Israel as the key event on the prophetic calendar, many dispensationalists have been aggressively moving the bar to the point of insisting that the restoration of Israel to "its original borders" is also necessary for prophetic fulfillment. They do not mean modest original borders of 1948 Israel, a territory smaller than its pre–1967 borders, but the borders of Israel at its height in biblical times.

In the view of many dispensationalists today, Israel must take over from the Palestinians all the territories of the West Bank, which Israeli settlers refer to as Judea and Samaria. Some push the borders even further, across into Jordan and to the Euphrates River, deep into Iraq.

While he bases his argument on Genesis rather than on Daniel or Revelation, Oklahoma Senator James Inhofe's remarks to the U.S. Senate in 2002 demonstrate the influence of this mentality on U.S. policymakers regarding present-day Israel and the occupied West Bank:

> I believe very strongly that we ought to support Israel; that it has a right to the land. . . . Because God said so. As I said a minute ago, look it up in the book of Genesis. It is right up there on the desk.
>
> In Genesis 13:14–17, the Bible says: "The Lord said to Abram, 'Lift up now your eyes, and look from the place where you are northward, and southward, and eastward and westward: for all the

land which you see, to you will I give it, and to your seed forever . . .
Arise, walk through the land in the length of it and in the breadth
of it; for I will give it to thee.'"

That is God talking.

The Bible says that Abram removed his tent and came and dwelt
in the plain of Mamre, which is in Hebron, and built there an altar
before the Lord. Hebron is in the West Bank. It is at this place
where God appeared to Abram and said, "I am giving you this
land," the West Bank.

This is not a political battle at all. It is a contest over whether or
not the word of God is true. (James Inhofe, "Seven Reasons Why
Israel Is Entitled to the Land," http://cbn.org/cbnnews/news/
020308c.html, accessed March 4, 2002)

The occupied city of Hebron in the West Bank, to which Senator Inhofe referred, is a place around which the competing interpretations of the biblical storyline contrast sharply. This ancient
city, with its tombs of the biblical Abraham and Sarah, is the second largest Palestinian city in the heart of the West Bank. It is also
the location of one of the most extreme and fanatical religious
Israeli settlements, largely drawn from immigrant American Jews.
These settlers seek to claim the city for Israelis even if that means
displacing Palestinians and bulldozing their homes.

The president of the right-wing Christian Coalition of America,
Roberta Combs, visited Hebron in 2002. She enthusiastically
embraced the Israeli settlers and advocated expansion of Israeli settlements throughout the West Bank as God's will for Israel.

Two weeks later, my husband and I went to Hebron to visit the
Christian Peacemaker Team, a mostly Mennonite and Church of
the Brethren group that has maintained a small nonviolent presence in old Hebron since 1995. The Christian peacemakers moni-

tor the tensions between Israeli settlers and more than 100,000 Palestinian residents, and they also seek to support Palestinians who are at risk of losing their homes and lands. Stationed in central Hebron are some 2000 Israeli soldiers whose job is to protect the 400 Israeli settlers. Confrontations are frequent. The Christian Peacemaker Team was invited to Hebron following the notorious 1994 massacre by American settler Baruch Goldstein, who opened fire on Muslim worshipers in the mosque at the Tomb of the Patriarchs, killing twenty-nine Palestinians and injuring scores more.

The bus dropped us off after dark in the center of old Hebron, the second largest city in the West Bank. Our two-hour ride from Jerusalem was on the same heavily armored bus that transports Israeli settlers deep into the West Bank. Most of the passengers got off at the settlement of Kiryat Arba, adjacent to Hebron, but we rode on past the Abraham Mosque or Tomb of the Patriarchs, into the old city. The streets were silent; it certainly looked and felt like a war zone. We heard the muted voices of Israeli soldiers huddled in their sandbagged outposts. Soldiers were the only people on the street, enforcing the twenty-four-hour curfew that had kept some 35,000 Palestinian residents under a kind of house arrest for hundreds of days.

Since I am a New Testament scholar, members of the Peacemaker team began to ask me questions about the biblical book of Revelation. Fundamentalist ideas have made their way into Mennonite churches and pulpits, though not the full-blown system of dispensationalism. Several of these volunteers were confused and hungry to understand the Bible, especially after the very public visit and statements of Christian Coalition leaders about biblical prophecy. "Does the Bible really say that Israel must control the whole land, as the settlers claim? Does Jesus really say the temple must be rebuilt, as fundamentalist Christians claim? Where are those biblical passages?"

The Bible does not say those things, I told them. But LaHaye and the Christian Coalition of America claim it does—in Revelation and Daniel. The Middle East is where their fictional end-times program becomes the most explosive. The Left Behind Web site asserts, "The veil between the fiction of *Left Behind* and the reality of life in the Middle East today is a thin one."

Faithful Christians today must challenge that notion of a "thin veil."

THE MIDDLE EAST END-TIMES SCRIPT

According to the dispensationalist view, the Bible not only foretells the re-establishment of greater Israel but also spells out a strict sequence of future geopolitical events that must happen in Israel and the Middle East as the world heads toward the end times. For example, Russia must invade Israel, according to most dispensationalists' interpretation of Ezekiel 38. This interpretation is based on the Hebrew word *rosh,* which they claim is an early name for Russia—a point that most Hebrew scholars view as ridiculous (since *rosh* actually means "head"). "Red China" with its "yellow peril" was Lindsey's original 1970 choice for the thermonuclear war he sees prophesied in Revelation 9, but he has recently shifted more emphasis to Arab invasions. His followers have to buy his revised editions to keep up on the latest biblical scenarios.

While the exact details of correlations vary as world events change, most prophecy enthusiasts agree on an overall sequence for the future. Specifically, the dispensationalist's script calls "these things" absolutely necessary for Jesus to come again to reign on earth:

- The rebirth of the nation of Israel;
- The Rapture of born-again Christians off the earth;

- The emergence of an evil Antichrist (and his one-world currency), probably from Europe;
- The Antichrist signs a seven-year peace treaty with Israel, setting in motion the seven years of tribulation—but the Antichrist will break the treaty after three and one half years;
- The rebuilding of the temple in Jerusalem and resumption of animal sacrifices there;
- The desecration of the temple by the evil Antichrist, followed by the second half of the seven-year period of tribulation;
- Jesus' return in the "Glorious Appearing" exactly seven years after the Rapture, beginning with his touch-down on the Mount of Olives, which will split the mountain into two.

According to their script, after Jesus wins the battle of Armageddon he will then set up his millennial kingdom from the throne of David in Jerusalem, and will reign for one thousand years over a kingdom repopulated by converted Jews and un-Raptured people left behind on earth. After that comes the last judgment, followed by eternity itself—God's New Jerusalem.

To this overall timetable individual authors add a host of other details from Revelation. And of course, much bloodshed, torture and violent death is required during every phase of the timetable, as spelled out in their reading of chapters 6–19 of Revelation.

TEMPLE REBUILDING FOR THE ANTICHRIST

According to this dispensationist script, the Rapture could happen at any moment, since there now is an Israeli state. But Christ cannot return again—the raging warrior Christ—until Jerusalem's Temple Mount is cleared of the Dome of the Rock and replaced with a new Jewish temple.

"There remains but one more event to completely set the stage for Israel's part in the last great act of her historical drama," writes Lindsey. "This is to rebuild the ancient temple of worship on its old site."[2]

The rebuilding of the temple is demanded, in their view, by that same passage from Daniel 9:26–27, the three verses of Scripture that dispensationalists say give God's framework for the world's entire prophetic future. The specific verse in question reads as follows: "He will make a firm covenant with the many for one week, but in the middle of the week he will put a stop to sacrifice and grain offering; and on the wing of abomination will come one who makes desolate."

"Temple" is not mentioned in this verse from Daniel, but "sacrifice" is. The only place Jews could sacrifice is in their Jerusalem temple. But priestly sacrifice ceased there in 70 A.D. when the Romans destroyed the temple in Jerusalem. Using this opaque verse from Daniel, dispensationalists claim that the temple must be rebuilt, because only if the temple is rebuilt can the Antichrist desecrate it halfway through the seven-year period of tribulation that they believe this verse foretells.

Most scholars think Daniel was originally writing about the desecration of the temple in 168 B.C. by Antiochus Epiphanes. In the New Testament, gospel writers again turned to this Daniel text and saw its fulfillment in Rome's traumatic desecration of the temple in 69–70 A.D.

But dispensationalist Christians view this text as still awaiting fulfillment in the future. Despite the fact that the Jewish temple has already twice been desecrated, they believe the Daniel prophecy requires that it be desecrated again. Since the temple has been in ruins since the Romans destroyed it in 70 A.D., the Antichrist cannot desecrate it unless it is rebuilt once more—not for its own sake nor for Jewish worship, but so that it can be desecrated one last time by the Antichrist in fulfillment of this prophecy from Daniel.

An article posted on the *Left Behind* Web page made clear this bizarre notion that the purpose of temple rebuilding is for its desecration:

> The End Times position portrayed in *Left Behind* (and explained further in the nonfiction companion *Are We In the End Times?*) includes the idea that before the Second Coming of Christ, Israel must be restored to its original borders and the temple must be rebuilt (in order for it to be desecrated by Antichrist).[3]

But dispensationalist arguments for temple rebuilding betray a blatant disregard for the New Testament and indeed, for Jesus' own words in the Gospel of John. Neither temple rebuilding nor the restoration of the nation of Israel is mandated in the New Testament. The clearest discussion of the Jewish temple in the New Testament is in chapter 2 of the Gospel of John, where the evangelist specifically states that the temple that will be rebuilt is the *temple of Jesus' resurrected body*—not the literal temple building itself: "Destroy this temple, and in three days I will raise it up," Jesus says. "The Jews then said, 'This temple has been under construction for forty-six years, and will you raise it up in three days?' But he was speaking of the temple of his body," the Gospel of John explains (John 2:20–21).

LaHaye and Lindsey largely ignore this passage from John 2. Others, such as Randall Price, argue that Jesus cannot be saying what he appears to be saying, since, in their view, it contradicts his teaching in the other Gospels.[4] Dispensationalists also ignore clear references in Revelation to the location of the temple "in heaven."[5] Nowhere does Revelation call for a literal temple to be rebuilt on earth.

The consequences of arguments for rebuilding the temple are extremely volatile for Middle East politics today. As Lindsey and other dispensationalists note, there is "one major problem" barring construction of a third Jewish temple—namely the Dome of the Rock. The third holiest site for Muslims, the Dome of the Rock has stood on the same site since the year 691 A.D. Along with the more recent Al Aqsa Mosque, the Dome of the Rock sits atop what is called the Haram Al Sharif or Noble Sanctuary by Muslims, the exact same site as the Temple Mount for Jews.

The Dome of the Rock is a beautifully proportioned octagonal building, with graceful columned arches covered by turquoise and blue tiles, crowned by a golden dome. Take off your shoes to go inside, and a sense of peace and tranquility surrounds you. The interior walls and columns are also turquoise and blue tiles. The whole octagonal edifice is built over a huge rock that protrudes into the center of the shrine. This beloved rock marks the very place where the prophet Muhammed is said to have ascended into heaven. This site is also venerated as the place where Abraham was miraculously spared from sacrificing his son.

In the view of Christian dispensationalists, however, this ancient octagonal building must be destroyed or moved. This is the only place the third temple can be built, says Lindsey—although in his recent writings he has determined that the Holy of Holies is not under the Muslim shrine but next to it, so that the two buildings theoretically could stand next to one another. "Obstacle or no obstacle, it is certain that the temple will be rebuilt. Prophecy demands it."[6]

Bullet holes in the blue and turquoise exterior tiles give a vivid reminder of one American Jewish extremist who, in 1982, took it upon himself to try to advance God's prophetic script by opening fire on the Dome of the Rock, using an M-16. An Australian Chris-

tian Zionist set fire to the Al Aqsa Mosque a few years earlier, with
the same goal of destroying the Muslim shrines in order to hasten
rebuilding of the temple. End times prophecy in the hands of
extremists can become a dangerous temptation—such people may
try to precipitate the required prophetic events themselves, "forcing God's hand," as Grace Halsell describes.[7]

There is little room for compromise when dealing with "prophecy." The stakes are high for dispensationalists. They bank their
entire hope for the Second Coming of Christ upon the rebuilt temple. Meanwhile, Muslims in Jerusalem and throughout the world
are understandably sensitive to political maneuvering and violent
incursions into their holy place. It is no accident that the second
Palestinian Intifada uprising is being called the "Al Aqsa Intifada,"
since many Muslims view Ariel Sharon's September 2000 visit to
the Temple Mount, accompanied by one thousand armed Israeli
soldiers, as not simply unwelcome but incendiary.

It is an understatement to call the question of rebuilding the
temple extremely volatile. The very idea that it could even be
raised as a question is astounding. *Left Behind* portrays Muslims as
voluntarily agreeing with the Antichrist's proposal to move the
Dome of the Rock to his capital city of "New Babylon" in Iraq, but
such a scenario is sheer dispensationalist fantasy. The shrine is the
most famous symbol of Jerusalem; the golden dome glows from
posters on the walls of almost every Arab restaurant you will ever
visit and in Muslim homes around the world.

Only a tiny minority of Messianic Jews support the temple
rebuilding concept. They are represented by fringe groups like the
Temple Institute, an organization in Jerusalem that is preparing
incense shovels, temple vessels and special priestly garments in
preparation for the day they can be used in a rebuilt temple. In the
strange alliances of Middle East politics today, these fringe Jews
come together with U.S.-based organizations of dispensationalist

Christians to work for the relocation or destruction of the Dome of the Rock and the rebuilding of the temple.

As Gershom Gorenberg points out in *The End of Days: Fundamentalism and the Struggle for the Temple Mount*, this is dangerous stuff today, impeding the fragile peace process in the Middle East.[8] Relocating or destroying the Dome of the Rock would bring certain cataclysm in the Muslim world. But dispensationalists are not interested in peace plans. Quite the opposite. They are eager for events to precipitate Jesus' second coming and set the prophetic end-times script in motion. Rebuilding the Jewish temple so the Antichrist can desecrate it is a required event in their prophetic countdown.

Fortunately, as Gorenberg also points out, a strange technicality makes it unlikely that animal sacrifice could resume even if a third temple were rebuilt. According to Numbers 19, only the ashes of a pure red heifer can cleanse a person from contact with human death. No one so tainted can enter the temple, yet no one can be purified of this uncleanness—which we are all presumed to have—unless they sprinkle themselves with a mixture of red heifer ashes and water. The technical difficulty is that no pure red heifer has been born in recent times; and the ashes of the last red heifer ran out in 70 A.D. American evangelical cattle breeders are eagerly trying to breed a pure red heifer, but have as yet been unsuccessful. For all practical purposes, temple sacrifice can never resume. Writes Gorenberg, "The absent ashes of the red heifer have a new function. They are a crucial factor in the political and strategic balance of the Middle East."[9]

NO LOVE OF THE JEWS

As an Israeli Jew, Gorenberg is highly critical of the *Left Behind* novels, and of the whole theology of dispensationalism. Christianity, Judaism, and Islam all have extremist fundamentalist strands that must be challenged, in his view, and *Left Behind* reflects the most dangerous element in Christianity. Gorenberg specifically points to the danger of anti-Semitism in dispensationalism. Speaking on *Sixty Minutes*, he observed, "They don't love real Jewish people. They love us as characters in their story, in their play, and that's not who we are . . . If you listen to the drama that they are describing, essentially, it's a five-act play in which the Jews disappear in the fourth act."[10]

Gorenberg is referring to the dispensationalist view that the only Jews who will survive the tribulation are those who convert to Christianity. Many politically pragmatic Israeli leaders are willing to accept both financial and political support from millions of dispensationalist Christian Zionists worldwide today regardless of their views that Jews who do not convert must finally die. Gorenberg, however, cautions against embracing such bedfellows. "People who see Israel through the lens of Endtimes prophecy are questionable allies." Their support can backfire when disappointed dispensationalists realize that Jews don't fit their script as they predicted, or when "Israel's real needs lead it to depart from the 'prophetic' program."[11]

NO LOVE FOR PALESTINIAN CHRISTIANS

If Jews play a disappearing role in the dispensationalist script, the role for Palestinians and Palestinian Christians is worse. Palestinian Christians do not even exist in the eyes of dispensationalists. "They do not view us as really Christian," explains Father Naim Ateek, an Anglican priest who founded and directs the Palestinian Liberation Theology Center Sabeel. "They call us cultural Christians only."

Ateek was a boy of eleven living in the town of Beisan (now Beth Shean) in 1948, when Jewish Haganah military forces entered their village and forced everyone to vacate their homes. "The soldiers separated us into two groups, Muslims and Christians. The

Muslims were sent across the Jordan River to the country of Transjordan (now Jordan). The Christians were taken on buses, driven to the outskirts of Nazareth, and dropped off there . . . Within a few hours, our family became refugees, driven out of Beisan forever."[12] Many Palestinians echo his story.

Christian Palestinians in the land today include Israeli citizens such as Ateek, as well as many others from the occupied West Bank and Gaza, who do not have Israeli citizenship. They are members of traditional churches whose presence in the region goes back centuries, even millennia—Greek Orthodox, Armenian Orthodox, Coptic Orthodox, Ethiopian Orthodox, Syrian Orthodox, Melkite, and Roman Catholic. These churches claim roots going all the way back to Pentecost, the event in the biblical book of Acts when the Holy Spirit descended on believers in Jerusalem. More recent Palestinian churches include Lutherans, Episcopalians, Anglicans, Baptists, and other evangelicals, whose presence dates to mission work in the nineteenth and twentieth centuries. Christians make up about 2 percent of the Palestinian population.

The influence of Palestinian Christians in Palestinian society is much greater than their numbers, thanks to the schools and hospitals they operate, the long history of their association with holy sites as well as other cultural factors. As *Boston Globe* correspondent Charles Sennott writes, "Historically, Christianity has provided a kind of leavening in the Middle East, a small but necessary ingredient acting as a buffer" between both Islamic and Israeli Jewish strands of ultranationalist fundamentalism.[13] But today, the Middle East's Christians' numbers are dwindling. Christians are squeezed by many forces. They long for partnership and solidarity with other Christians internationally—a partnership they do get from Anglicans, Lutherans, Roman Catholics and other churches around the world.

But they will not find that solidarity with Christian Zionists. Dispensationalist tours bring plane-loads of American Christians to the Holy Land, but they never encounter Father Ateek or any of the other indigenous Palestinian Christians of the region. Halsell describes participating in two such trips led by Jerry Falwell, each with hundreds of participants. "Christians were all around us, tens of thousands of them. But Falwell did not arrange for us to meet Christians."[14] Dispensationalist tours focus exclusively on biblical holy sites and Israeli monuments, completely overlooking the Christians who have lived in the region for millennia.

In the dispensationalist view, God's promises do not apply to Christians who are currently living in the land, who have faithfully gathered for prayer and cared for the Christian holy sites and whose claims to the land go back many generations.

Evangelical professor Timothy Weber calls it "ironic" that in the "flush of prophetic fulfillment" since Israel's birth in 1948 most evangelicals have shown little or no concern for Palestinians—given the number of Palestinian Christians and other Arab Christians in the Middle East.[15] The fact is that the Christian church in the Middle East is Arab. These Christians are ignored in the dispensationalist script because they do not fit neatly into Darby's end-times prophetic scenario. Weber's historical overview of "How Evangelicals Became Israel's Best Friend" demonstrates how closely intertwined the history of Israel's birth was with the history of dispensationalism.

Another evangelical leader who decries evangelicals' lack of support for local Palestinian churches is Richard Mouw, president of Fuller Seminary in Pasadena, California. While he supports Israel and its role in biblical prophecy, Mouw notes that "it is unfortunate that the impression is often given by evangelicals that the struggle in the Middle East is basically one between Jews and Muslims. This ignores the plight of thousands of members of the Christian churches in that region."[16]

Mouw and a number of prominent evangelical leaders, including author Philip Yancey and editor of *Christianity Today* David
Neff, sent an open letter of concern to President George W. Bush
in July 2002 urging him to support a more even-handed Middle
East policy. They emphasized that they and many other American
evangelicals "reject the way some have distorted biblical passages
as their rationale for uncritical support for every policy and action
of the Israeli government." The letter's signers urge the president
to judge the actions of both Israelis and Palestinians "on the basis
of biblical standards of justice." The letter also endorses the long-
time U.S. position of support for a Palestinian state within 1967
borders.[17]

The most extreme right-wing Christians go further than ignoring Palestinian Christians. They actually adopt the perspective that
Palestinian Christians, along with all other Palestinians, must be
relocated to Jordan—so that Israel can take over the entire West
Bank, as promised in the Bible.

In *Israel in Crisis: What Lies Ahead*, prophecy author David
Dolan's compassionate tone belies his extreme views. God promised to give the entire "hill country" to Israel, Dolan argues, as
specified in the prophet Jeremiah. These hills are the West Bank,
recognized as Palestinian territory by the United States and United Nations and all countries of the world. But U.N. resolutions
and international law are no match for the Bible. In Dolan's view,
God is fulfilling the prophecy of Jeremiah 31 today by giving the
West Bank to Israel, taking it away from the Palestinians who
have lived there for millennia. Palestinians who want to stay in
their homes must be willing to live under Israeli sovereignty, as
the Bible specifies for strangers and aliens living in Israel. For
Palestinians who do not want to live under Israel the only option
is "transfer."[18]

It's all prophecied in the Bible, so these folks say.

POST-1967 U.S. CHRISTIAN SUPPORT FOR ISRAEL, THE OCCUPATION, AND SETTLEMENTS

Enthusiasm for the State of Israel among U.S. Christians escalated rapidly after the 1967 war, when Israel gained control of East Jerusalem, the Old City (including the Western Wall of the ancient temple area), the Gaza Strip and the West Bank—a significant geographical area west of the Jordan River, formerly administered by Jordan. Dispensationalists' fervor was soon combined with opportunism as evangelists gathered hundreds of people for rallies in Israel, initiated festivals for born-again Christians in Israel, advocated for political candidates, donated money and voiced their opinions on U.S. foreign policy. Eventually U.S. Christians were even raising money to relocate American Jews in Israel.[19]

The campaign, which begins with misinterpreting biblical prophecy, does not stop there. The prophecy industry has many informal franchises, and its leaders are interested in the political, commercial, economic, and military angles on the coming kingdom. Now in a strange but close relationship with the government of Israel, Christian Zionist groups are deeply involved in Israeli political life, with goals of aiding Israel in achieving regional dominance, control of water resources, and more.

This alliance has encouraged the government of Israel to continue its occupation of West Bank areas by force, to expand its settlements, and to squeeze resident Palestinians more and more tightly into impossibly restrictive districts.

It is very important for well-meaning U.S. Christians to get a picture of what such a misguided "prophetic program" means for real people. What does occupation look like for Palestinians in the West Bank, Gaza, and East Jerusalem? What does it feel like for the Israeli soldiers and citizens who are called upon to justify and enforce it?

In the occupied lands, Palestinian people are almost completely immobilized. Israel has routinely blocked the movement of residents of the cities and villages and refugee camps by simply destroying the roads. The highways are ruined with trenches 8 feet deep and 15 feet wide, or with 10-foot-high earth roadblocks bulldozed over the pavement. People of the West Bank and Gaza cannot move freely over the old roads, and they are also forbidden to drive on the newly built thoroughfares leading to Israeli settlement towns. A "separation wall" is the latest barrier. A map of the West Bank looks like Swiss cheese, with Palestinians living only in the holes.

Military checkpoints impede movement at almost every juncture, and the soldiers on duty may use their own discretion to delay or harass the people—or to let them pass. Proper documents are required, but often a Palestinian's proper documentation does not mean a thing.

A Palestinian Christian pastor from Beit Sahour—the "Shepherd's Field" of the Gospel of Luke's Christmas story, located near Bethlehem and very close to Jerusalem—tells of the excitement in his young family as the day approached for his eldest son's high school graduation. The commencement ceremony was to be at his son's academy in Jerusalem, so the pastor made sure he had the proper permit to travel there on that date. On that spring day, with four children and their mother all dressed up for such an important occasion, the first-born son in his first grown-man suit, the pastor drove toward Jerusalem. Soldiers stopped the car at the Bethlehem checkpoint and refused to allow the family to pass. The pastor showed his permit, then his clergy identification card, but these made no difference. He pleaded with the soldiers, pointing again and again to his permit and the date indicated, finally asking them just to look into the car and see his proud and beautiful family, his young son. They were not moved.

In defeat the pastor turned his car around and drove his family home. His wife prepared some treats and they invited neighbors and members of their congregation to help them celebrate their son's achievement. How will that young man remember his graduation day? By recalling his father humiliated and begging at the checkpoint? His little sisters wide-eyed with fear, his young brother tearful and angry? His mother, trying to salvage his coming-of-age day with a homespun party?

Every Palestinian can tell you a similar story of humiliation at checkpoints, or stories that are much worse. Humiliation and harassment are daily facts of life under occupation. Pregnant women in labor have been turned back at checkpoints, only to have their babies die because they were kept from hospitals. The occupation is bringing about a deep hopelessness and rage among Palestinians who are unable to get to their jobs or to school, unable to visit sick family members or reach a hospital, unable to leave their homes at all when curfews are imposed for days on end.

"SETTLEMENTS" AND BIBLICAL PROPHECY

There is no consensus in Israel on the value of the occupation of Gaza, the West Bank, and East Jerusalem. The term "settlements" refers to Israeli residences built on land occupied by Israel in the 1967 war. These settlements are considered illegal under international law, since according the Geneva Conventions an occupying force is not permitted to move any of its own population permanently into occupied territories.[20] Israel, on the other hand, calls these lands "disputed." The existence of these settlements in the West Bank, Gaza, and East Jerusalem are a source of great resentment and hostility for Palestinians who watch more and more of their land being annexed by settlers or settler roads or separation barriers seemingly every day.

Polls show that most Israelis feel the long-held policy of occupation and of locating 400,000 Israeli settlers in the territories is a serious liability for Israel. In November 2003 a public opinion poll conducted by the James A. Baker III Institute for Public Policy at Rice University in Houston and the International Crisis Group found that a majority of Israelis would support a peace plan that includes dismantling most settlements and establishing a Palestinian state within 1967 border, with adjustments around Jerusalem.[21] Popular support for concessions is also reflected in the grass-roots movement, "The People's Voice," initiated by a former Israeli intelligence chief and a prominent Palestinian leader that had garnered more than 200,000 signatures of support among both Israelis and Palestinians as of December 2003.[22] Citizens on both sides want peace, and most Israelis are willing to give back territory and dismantle settlements in exchange for peace.

Perhaps the most hopeful sign is the "Geneva Initiative," an unofficial yet landmark fifty-page Israeli/Palestinian peace agreement signed December 1, 2003, by former ministers Yossi Beilin of Israel and Yasser Abed Rabbo of the Palestinian Authority. The agreement is similar to the terms a majority of Israelis and Palestinians tell pollsters they would support. Says Beilen of the Geneva Initiative, "We are saying to the world: 'Don't believe those who tell you that our conflict is unsolvable . . . Help us to end it.'"

Yet a critical mass of American dispensationalist Christians are committed to the principle of occupation and in some cases devoted to particular settlements, a sure recipe prolonging the conflict. Christian Friends of Israeli Communities[23] is a Colorado group that links U.S. evangelical congregations with Israeli settlements. Their stance is that "Bible-believing people throughout the world can truly understand the importance of these communities and how vital it is that they continue to grow and thrive. Christians the world over are called to stand up for these communities and for the brave people that live there." The entire premise for this organization is based in their dispensationalist interpretation of biblical prophecy. "The prophets foretold the ingathering of the exiles and the rebuilding of the Land in the latter days," they state.

These evangelical Christians consider all the lands formerly entirely Palestinian—of which Palestinians now have only a fraction (and a diminishing fraction) for their own towns, farms and homes—to belong to Israel. Only recently have some areas been "reunited" with Israel:

> In 1948, Israel was reborn as a sovereign nation and in 1967 the "West Bank" was reunited with the rest of the nation in the prophetic, miraculous Six Day War . . . The land remained barren until the Jews returned to cultivate it. This is truly the fulfillment of prophecy. (Christian Friends of Israeli Communities, http://www.cfoic.com)

Why are Americans so ready to identify with extremist settlers in Israel? Why is the expansionist version of prophecy such a powerful draw for U.S. Christians? The Rev. John Hubers of the Reformed Church in America posits that to many Americans modern Israelis look like the wilderness-busting pioneers of the U.S. frontier. Writing in *Newsreport*, a publication of the Middle East Council of Churches, he suggests:

> One explanation for the tenacious hold of the dispensationalist myth on the American consciousness (even beyond evangelical circles)—it echoes themes of the American frontier myth. We hear

our own story in Israel's story. We identify with the Zionists because their experience matches ours. (John Hubers, "Christian Zionism and the Myth of America," *Newsreport*, Autumn 2002; http://www.cmep.org/theology/2003may9.htm)

Whatever the reason, we need to change the lens through which Americans read the biblical story in the Middle East. *Left Behind* is a fictional world; so, too, is the "dispensationalist myth" on which it is based.

It is a fictional Christian script with potent and dangerous consequences for both Israelis and Palestinians.

WORLD WAR III AND ETHNIC CLEANSING

World War III is more than a bit player in the dispensationalist script. Its onset is supposed to be cause for rejoicing among true Christians.

John Hagee, pastor of Cornerstone Church in San Antonio, told a BBC interviewer that World War III has already begun. "We are seeing in my judgment the birthpangs that will be called in the future the beginning of the end. I believe in my mind that the Third World War has already begun. I believe it began on 9/11."

Hagee continues, "I believe we are going to see an escalation of the Islamic influence all over the earth, and at that point in time God in his sovereign grace is going to stand up and defend Israel, and the enemies of Israel are going to be decimated."

The interviewer asked Hagee whether he thought some listeners might find his view of global confrontation inflammatory or dangerous. "No," Hagee replied, "it's not dangerous. When you know the future there's no reason to consider it inflammatory. *It's going to happen.*"[24]

Hagee is not the only one to invoke imagery of September 11, or even World War III, in connection with the Bible. A Time/CNN poll found that 59 percent of Americans say they believe the events in Revelation are going to come true, and nearly one-quarter think the Bible predicted the September 11 attack.[25] As reported in *Time's* cover story on "The Bible & the Apocalypse," 36 percent of Americans polled who support Israel "say they do so because they believe in biblical prophecies that Jews must control Israel before Christ will come again." Although the report does not specify whether "Israel" includes the West Bank in this poll, the numbers are nonetheless significant. If more than one-third of those polled invoke this definition of biblical prophecy in support of a particular and absolutist Middle East political scenario, this is frightening—especially when that belief translates into unquestioning support for U.S. military and political aid, including expansion of Israel's settlements.

For some, it even justifies a form of ethnic cleansing—transferring Palestinians out of their homeland. Such is the view of former U.S. House Republican Majority Leader Dick Armey, a fundamentalist Christian from Texas. Speaking on MSNBC's program *Hardball* in May 2002, Armey said he believes that "there are many Arab nations that have many hundreds of thousands of acres of land, soil and property and opportunity to create a Palestinian state." That is where Palestinians should go, in Armey's view.

When pressed by the incredulous interviewer Chris Matthews whether he really meant that Palestinians should leave the West Bank, Armey explained that yes, "most of the people who now populate Israel were transported from all over the world to that land and they made it their home. The Palestinians can do the same."[26]

CHALLENGING THE WAR SCRIPT
AND VIOLENT EXTREMISM

I want to be perfectly clear that what I am challenging is not Zionism but *Christian* Zionism, with its absolutist war script for the Middle East and for the end of the world. Many Israelis also challenge this phenomenon. As Yossi Alfer, former Israeli intelligence agent and Israel, director of the American Jewish Committee, said on CBS's *Sixty Minutes* feature "Zion's Christian Soldiers," "God save us from these people."

It is important to be clear on this distinction regarding Zionism, since the legacy of Christians in terms of anti-Judaism and anti-Semitism has been so shameful. We and our churches must confess the sin of anti-Judaism and repent—as did my own Evangelical Lutheran Church in America when it repudiated Martin Luther's anti-Jewish writings. [27] We must also condemn all violence, including Palestinian suicide attacks against Israelis. Supporting Jews and Judaism is one of the most important things Christians and biblical scholars can do, and this includes supporting the state of Israel and its right to exist within secure pre-1967 borders.

But that is different from supporting a dispensationalist formula that links Christian faith to expelling Palestinians from their homeland today, as Rep. Armey advocated. Whenever people invoke biblical prophets to support a program of violence or injustice, this is a misuse of the Bible. This is extremism.

Falwell called the prophet Muhammed a "terrorist" and a "violent man of war," singling out Islam as an inherently violent religion. [28] But Judaism, Christianity, and Islam can *all* be characterized as religions of violence—and all three are also religions of peace. It depends on which strands you tease out from each tradition, since each also has a violent, even "terrorist," strand in its legacy, as well as core scriptures and traditions that call for peace-making.

My point is this: We cannot afford to give in to those violent strands in our biblical tradition. We must say "No" to the dispensationalists' distorted claims that the book of Revelation is God's battle plan for the end. Their view has disastrous consequences for us all, especially in Jerusalem and the Middle East. The storyline dedicated to war must not have the last word. It is not the heart of the Bible nor is it the heart of God.

What is needed is to counter the Christian Zionist myth with real-life stories of Palestinians who suffer under the occupation, stories of Israelis who feel they are losing the soul of their country, and also stories of the many Israelis and Palestinians who are working for justice and peace. The importance of stories was a recurring theme that Duke University researcher Amy Johnson Frykholm heard in interviews with *Left Behind* readers about the appeal of the novels. One avid fan of the novels, "Rachel," told Frykholm that only "another story" would convince her to rethink her devotion to the dispensationalist version of end-times.[29] Well, we *do* have another story to tell Rachel. We have the stories of the power of nonviolence and reconciliation among Israelis and Palestinians. We also have Revelation's story of Lamb power—the biblical story of a God who gives a place at the table to all peoples.

The Palestinian Lutheran bishop in Jerusalem, Munib Younan, believes that Christians can be a prophetic "axis of hope" to counter absolutist rhetoric of an axis of evil. His own story of growing up as a refugee in Jerusalem's Old City shapes his theology of peace in significant ways.[30] Younan envisions a "prophetic" presence—using the definition of prophecy not in the dispensationalist sense of prediction but rather as God's call to be a voice for justice and one who critiques injustice:

The Palestinian Church is also called to be an axis of hope and to be prophetic. It is called to condemn injustice but at the same time to bring hope, work for justice, and prepare a generation of hope and peace. We do this by treating people justly at home and at work, raising our children to trust in Jesus Christ as our Savior, living just and peaceful lives. We do this by teaching justice and peace in our Lutheran and Christian schools, and practicing justice, peace and reconciliation in our congregations . . . The Christian church needs to be prophetic in order to break the vicious cycle of hatred and revenge. ("Bishop Younan's Reformation Day Message," in Ann E. Hafften, ed., *Water from the Rock: Lutheran Voices from Palestine* [Minneapolis, Minn.: Fortress Press, 2003], 22)

The story of Yehezkel and Dalia Landau is another story that teaches hope. Yehezkel Landau is the Israeli theologian who questioned President Reagan's view of prophecy in the Middle East in 1983. The Landaus are peace advocates, working for an end to Israel's occupation of the West Bank and for a two-state solution. They are also religious Zionists—Jews whose vision for Zionism includes a place for Palestinians as full partners in God's story.[31] The biblical story that shapes their view of the Middle East and the world is a prophetic vision—a version of the story that ends not in Armageddon but rather in a shared peace, a shared Jerusalem.

Dalia's own personal story is compelling. In 1967, she discovered that the house in which she grew up in Ramle, Israel, was the house of an Arab family who had been forcibly evacuated by the Israeli army in 1948. When Dalia was just a baby her family had taken up residence in what they thought was an "abandoned" home. Almost twenty years later, after Israel's 1967 occupation of the West Bank, she met the al-Khayri family when they came back and asked to visit their house. When her parents died, Dalia inherited the house and decided to donate it to found the organization Open House, a center for healing and reconciliation between Israeli Jews and Israeli Arabs. The center brings together Palestinian and Israeli young people to share dreams and stories, and to work as peacemakers.[32]

There are a host of other stories we could lift up to counteract the absolutist and violent story of Christian Zionism in the Middle East—the story of Naim Ateek and Sabeel, the liberation theology center whose Arabic name means "spring of water"; the story of the Israeli Committee Against House Demolitions where Israelis and Palestinians work side by side to rebuild bulldozed houses; the story of Women in Black, whose silent protests against occupation bring a courageous witness year after year; the story of churches from around the world partnering with Palestinian churches as well as seeking to understand Judaism more fully; the story of Rabbis for Human Rights; the story of B'Tselem, a Hebrew word for "in the image of," an organization that monitors human rights violations and seeks to change Israeli policy. Most of all, we can tell the stories of regular people, Palestinians and Israelis, who don't want to be disposable players in someone's end-times script. They simply want to live their lives at peace with their neighbors.

Israel, the West Bank, Gaza, and Jerusalem have no lack of people who believe that God wants them to live together in peace, not war. We need to lift up their stories for a different vision of Zionism—and a different vision of Christianity.

But listen now to the best alternative story of all.

O LITTLE TOWN OF BETHLEHEM

Come with me on a journey to Bethlehem. To the place where Lamb power was born in our world and laid in a humble stable crib some two thousand years ago, the place where God came to dwell in our world in Jesus and has never left the world behind.

In the end, it is only this story of Jesus' birth as a tiny child in Bethlehem that can counter the violent, avenging story the Christian Zionists love to tell. Rather than rallying the troops in Jerusalem in anticipation of the lion-like Jesus' end-times return to fight the mother of all battles, rather than craving the violence, we can say with the shepherds of Luke's Gospel, "let us go over to Bethlehem." In Bethlehem you meet the Lamb Jesus whose birth you can comprehend only by stooping low to the ground, in humility and wonder. In Bethlehem, today as in the time of Christ, we can learn a different story—not the violent war but the story of Jesus who was born in a manger.

The Church of the Nativity in Bethlehem marks the spot where Jesus was born, according to tradition. The church has been the site of so much violence, most recently when Palestinians who had taken refuge inside were under siege from Israeli tanks and troops. The birthplace of the prince of peace also has a long history of sheltering people from violence. Pastor Mitri Raheb, pastor of Christmas Lutheran Church in Bethlehem, recalls how his family sought shelter there in 1967:

> I can still remember the Six Day War in 1967; shortly after war broke out and Israel started shelling Bethlehem, my mother carried me to the Church of the Nativity, where we and many other Christian families from Bethlehem found refuge. We all lived together in the rooms of the church for the duration of the war. This is where we felt safe and secure despite the bombardments. (Mitri Raheb, *I Am a Palestinian Christian* [Minneapolis, Minn.: Fortress Press, 1995], 4)

You bend down low to enter the door into the Church of the Nativity and you bend even lower to touch the place on the floor where Christ was born. A star marks the spot. Christians from around the world come to see and kiss that star, to marvel at the birth of healing in our world in Jesus. Jesus came as a tiny baby, vulnerable and dependent, God incarnate in our world. He came in love and healing. He spent his whole life healing people and even gave his life for our wounded world.

There are many, many wounds in Palestine and Israel today—countless wounds caused by the daily brutality of military occupation as well as by suicide bombings, and by the long history of suffering for these peoples. I have seen those wounds. But I have also seen amazing care and healing, in the work of nurses and doctors and physical therapists and the many others who risk their lives to care for people's wounds.

On Christmas Eve Day, 2002, I met a wonderful nurse in Bethlehem who reminded me of God's care for our world's wounds. Because of curfews we were not able to get to Bethlehem until the very last week of our month-long visit. Finally on Christmas Eve, when the Israeli military briefly lifted its curfew in Bethlehem, we were able to enter this city of Christ's birth. As soon as we walked through the Bethlehem checkpoint and into town the mood was jubilant. Despite the rain, people rejoiced that they could go out of their houses after weeks of being cooped up.

We joined a silent demonstration against the Israeli occupation in Manger Square, along with Christians from Bethlehem and around the world and Israeli "Peace Now" demonstrators, just outside the Church of the Nativity. It was there, as we stood in the cold rain, holding our "End the Occupation" signs and huddling to keep warm that we met the Palestinian nurse, a Greek Orthodox Christian, who invited us home to his family's house for lunch.

The family's hospitality was gracious despite the hardships of occupation. They showed us where Israeli soldiers had beaten down the door of their one-room house in Bethlehem's Old City, looking for terrorists. What impressed me most was to hear the Palestinian nurse describe his work and his love for patients, most of whom are Israelis. His specialty is wound care, although he has lost his job at Hadassah Hospital in Jerusalem because he can't get there due to Bethlehem closures and curfew. Now he raises chickens. He has gentle eyes and a gentle manner.

As I listened to his descriptions of tending patients' wounds and coaxing them to heal, I recognized the names of some of the same dressings that had held my own leg together when I fell in a hiking accident earlier in the year. That connection to my own wound was very moving. It was a reminder of how deeply we are all connected, both in our wounds and in our capacity for healing. Here was a Palestinian nurse who loves to care for people, who seeks only the opportunity to bring God's healing love to people's excruciating wounds.

The care the nurse spoke of is the same care Jesus gave to wounded people wherever he went—to Peter's mother-in-law, to the bent-over woman, to people possessed by fevers and demons, as he laid his hands on them, lifting them up. The whole Bible is full of amazing pictures for the healing of the world. This is the care God wants to give to the Israeli/Palestinian situation today, and to our entire world.

What is the message of the book of Revelation as we ponder the situation in the Middle East today? As I think about wounds in Israel or Palestine in light of the book of Revelation, I keep coming back to Revelation's promise of the healing "tree of life" (Rev 22:2). The tree of life is Revelation's most powerful image—first promised in Revelation to fulfill people's hunger, and then brought to life in chapter 22 as a magnificent world-healing tree with "leaves for the healing of the nations." This vision comes from the Old Testament prophet Ezekiel, who envisioned a similar wondrous tree with leaves for healing (Ezek 47:9–12). The tree of life is also an important image in Islamic tradition.

I believe that God is inviting us to take to heart not the dispensationalists' violent version of the biblical story, not Armageddon, but the Bible's amazing vision of the tree of life and its healing for the world. Just like that nurse in Bethlehem who is so gifted at wound care, God is laying healing leaves on our world's wounds today, and coaxing people back to healing despite their most painful divisions.

The message of Revelation for the Middle East is not that God plans to destroy the world with a bloody battle culminating in Jerusalem, but rather the vision and promise of New Jerusalem: the story of a shared city, with a tree of life and open gates to welcome all nations.

The biblical tree of life proclaims the same message as the story of Jesus' birth in a lowly, straw-filled manger in Bethlehem: that God comes into the world to bring peace and healing to the Middle East, to all nations, and to all creation.

Prophecy and Apocalypse

PEOPLE ARE ENDLESSLY CURIOUS about the biblical book of Revelation. Yet when they actually sit down to read Revelation they often find it intimidating and difficult. *The Late Great Planet Earth* and the *Left Behind* novels make Revelation accessible. That is a big part of their appeal. The novels are written for "people who don't want to read Revelation," says a 27-year-old fan of *Left Behind* who likes the soap-opera quality of the series. The authors are "trying to make it easy and fun."[1]

The problem is that the whole dispensationalist system these books use to make Revelation easy and fun is a fabrication. It is based on a false view of prophecy. This chapter will examine and challenge elements of that fabrication, especially the claim that Revelation gives us God's play-by-play prophetic script for the future.

The very first word in Revelation is "apocalypse," usually translated as "revelation." What is an apocalypse? What does this word tell us about the meaning of the book? Contrary to common association of the word with end-times disasters or cataclysm, the word apocalypse means "unveiling." Apocalypses pull back a curtain to unveil or reveal some deep truth about the world. When Revelation was written, apocalypse was a popular type of literature for Jews and Christians. Apocalypses were easy for ancient readers to understand because people were familiar with the structure and imagery, just as we are familiar with science fiction and horror movies today. People in the ancient world were drawn to the drama and mystery of apocalypses.

One typical element of Revelation and many other ancient apocalypses is the visionary journey. This journey can involve both time-travel and space-travel. A person travels out into the future or back into the past, up to heaven or down into the underworld. Along the journey the traveler encounters angels and shape-shifting animals in mysterious colors, battles, coronations, and other scenes of terrifying and life-changing power. In one apocalypse, "Second Esdras," in the biblical apocrypha, Ezra goes on an apocalyptic journey and meets a twelve-winged eagle, a talking lion, and a weeping woman who turns into a city. Revelation's talking altar, multiheaded beasts, woman-cities and other fantastic creatures are not at all unusual for an apocalyptic journey.

In a typical apocalypse the traveling visionary returns from the journey with an urgent message for us about what he or she has seen—usually a call for repentance and faithfulness, perhaps also a political critique like the talking lion who decries the Roman empire for its injustice in Second Esdras. One of the Dead Sea Scrolls texts is an apocalypse, as is the biblical book of Daniel. Martha Himmelfarb's book *Tours of Hell* surveys these underworld journeys in several ancient apocalypses.[2]

One hundred years ago Charles Dickens wrote about an apocalyptic journey in his well-known *A Christmas Carol*—a morality play in which the miserly Scrooge is taken on a visionary tour of his life. A hair-raising visit from the ghost of his dead business partner,

Jacob Marley, gives Scrooge the first warning of what his future will be if he does not change his life. Marley drags chains made of "cash-boxes, keys, padlocks, ledgers, deeds, and heavy purses wrought in steel." Subsequent visitations by three spirits show Scrooge his painful past and his even more painful future. He also sees a scene that inspires hope—the warmth and love of the Cratchit house. These contrasting visions prove to be a wake-up call for Scrooge.

Scrooge is changed by the final vision, when he sees his own lonely grave. He pleads with the Spirit of Christmas Future: Let the visions only show what *"may* be," so he can still hope to change his terrifying future:

> The Spirit stood among the graves, and pointed down to one. [Scrooge] advanced towards it trembling . . . "Before I draw nearer to that stone to which you point," said Scrooge, "answer me one question. Are these the shadows of the things that Will be, or are they shadows of things that May be, only?"
>
> Still the Ghost pointed downward to the grave by which it stood . . .
>
> "Spirit!" he cried, tight clutching at its robe, "Hear me! I am not the man I was. I will not be the man I must have been but for this intercourse. Why show me this, if I am past all hope?"
>
> For the first time the hand appeared to shake.
>
> "Good Spirit," he pursued, as down upon the ground he fell before it: "Your nature intercedes for me, and pities me. Assure me that I yet may change these shadows you have shown me, by an altered life!" (www.literature.org/authors)

In the terrifying moment when he sees a vision of his own grave, Scrooge alters his life. Assured that what he sees does not have to come to pass, he commits to walking a different path. Scrooge awakes to realize that he is still in bed. He has been on a visionary journey that has changed him forever.

The book of Revelation takes its readers on journeys that function in a similar way. The visionary world of Revelation is different from *A Christmas Carol*, to be sure, but both books employ the motifs of apocalyptic journeys. John, the author of Revelation, is taken on a series of visionary journeys on behalf of his seven churches. Transported out into the future, he is shown contrasting visions of two cities. He sees the evil whore called "Babylon," whose merchants and kings lament the loss of all their wealth. He hears that Babylon sits on seven hills—identifying Rome—and he hears the voice of an angel calling Christians to reject Rome and all that it represents: "come out of her, my people" (Rev 18:4).

Finally John sees an alternative city—God's wonderful paradise-like world, descending from heaven like a bride, inviting us in. This is the citizenship Christians are to hope for. The urgent message is that Christians must be faithful in worshiping God and renounce Babylon/Rome in order to participate in God's holy city.[3]

In the first of his apocalyptic journeys (Rev 4–5) John travels up to heaven. There he sees a beautiful vision of God's throne, revealed to be the true power behind the universe. Angels and animals are worshiping God and singing songs of praise to Jesus, the Lamb. Revelation's subsequent visions pull back the curtain to "unveil" the Roman empire for what it really is: Rome is not the great eternal power it claims to be, but a demonic beast that oppresses the world. God's people must undertake a spiritual exodus out of the empire, led by the Lamb. God threatens evil Babylon/Rome with plagues like the plagues of the Exodus story. We must not put our trust in Roman security or power, nor that of any other empire. We are to give allegiance to God alone.

Like all apocalypses, Revelation terrifies us with scenes of destruction. Over the course of its twenty-two chapters readers travel through earthquakes, oceanic plagues, and unthinkable human and natural disasters. Specific details of Revelation's sequences of seven seals, trumpets, and bowls and their calamitous plagues are part of the book's wake-up call to us. They function like Scrooge's terrifying visions, their vivid details inspiring readers to repent. The threat to Scrooge was not that he would end up dragging literal chains made of cash-boxes, keys, and padlocks. He was bound by the chains in his life and his heart. The visions' realism made them fearful, but not as literal prediction for the future. Similarly, Revelation's primary purpose is life-changing; it does not predict literal events. The book's goal is to exhort us to faithfulness to God by means of a new vision.

Scrooge's question to the Spirit is the right one to ask about Revelation's visions as well: "Why show me this, if I am past all hope?" The book of Revelation—like *A Christmas Carol*—shows us terrifying visions precisely because there *is* still hope for us and for the earth. Indeed, the hope of the book of Revelation is that God's Lamb, Jesus, is already victorious and that God's people will be faithful to the Bible's vision of life. The hope is that we will follow the Lamb, renouncing all the seductions of imperial injustice and violence, so the threat of the plagues will be averted. God loves the world. God does not desire earth's destruction.

Jesus tells a vivid apocalyptic story in the Gospel of Luke, with a goal similar to that of Revelation and Dickens's *A Christmas Carol*. In the story, a fabulously rich man died after a lifetime of ignoring the sufferings of a poor man, Lazarus, who begs at his gate. Now the man is suffering punishment. Jesus takes us first on a journey to Hades to see the rich man's gruesome agonies. A contrasting heavenly vision then shows us Lazarus's blessedness in Abraham's bosom. The apocalyptic contrast is all the more vivid because the rich man can also see Lazarus in far off heaven and begs for Lazarus to come to comfort him. But the message of the story is contained in Abraham's counsel to the rich man, which we over-hear: "Remember that during your lifetime you received your good things and Lazarus in like manner evil things; but now he is com-forted here, and you are in agony" (Luke 16:25).

The purpose of Jesus' story is not to predict the details of actu-al future sufferings or blessings. Abraham's bosom is not a literal place, after all! Jesus tells the story as a wake-up call for those who are still alive, helping us to see the poor at our gate and do some-thing before it is too late, before the terrifying chasm is fixed. Jesus wants to warn his audience about the consequences of fail-ing to care for the poor, and also of failing to recognize the pres-ence of the Messiah in their midst. For us, the terrifying visionary journeys to Hades and heaven awaken a sense of urgency about our situation.

The *Left Behind* novels follow the pattern of other apocalypses as they take readers on a vivid journey and wake them up to a sense of urgency about God. That is the novels' strength. Their failing is the dangerous conclusions about God and our life in the world that grow out of the *Left Behind* version of the apocalyptic journey. *Left Behind* presents an individualistic, jet-setting life for its secret band of born-again "Tribulation Force" heroes, a lifestyle that stands in sharp contrast to the Bible's concern for the hungry and the poor, as Jesus taught in Luke 16. *Left Behind*'s characters spend more time in airplanes and helicopters, or in underground bunkers, than they do walking the earth —illustrating the dispensationalist view of the world as a place from which to escape. Their high-tech gear, satellite phones, customized Range Rovers and stadium-size rallies cannot be reconciled with the heart of Revelation, because more than any other biblical book Revelation speaks to marginalized and powerless people.

Revelation was originally written for those whom South African theologian Allan Boesak calls "God's little people"—communities of people who struggled under oppression—not for people with access to airplanes or money or the latest technology. The best way to understand Revelation's message for today is to put ourselves in the place of the audience for whom it was originally written. Imagine Revelation as a message from the underside, written to comfort beleaguered churches struggling under Roman imperial violence and power. Revelation has spoken powerfully to oppressed people throughout history. Its voice of protest is heard in spirituals as well as gospel songs and hymns.

When Revelation was written, the memory of the terrible Jewish War of 68–70 A.D. was fresh in everyone's mind. Just two decades earlier, Roman conquerors had burned Jerusalem and enslaved or exiled the Jewish people. John, the author of Revelation, might have been a refugee from that war. John wrote from Patmos, an island off the coast of Western Turkey, around the year 96 A.D. His goal was to help people see, to unveil the truth about the world. His apocalypse spoke a daring word, pulling back the curtain to expose Rome's brutality and illegitimacy.

Most daring of all is Revelation's declaration that Rome would only last "a little while longer" and that its end would come soon. For its original first-century audience, Revelation's proclamation of an impending "end" referred not to the end of the world but to the end of Roman rule. Revelation confronts Rome's own slogan of *Roma Aeterna* ("Eternal Rome") with a bold word of prophecy and critique. The ancient format of apocalypse linked John's critique to other apocalyptic biblical critiques of unjust empires. John was pulling back the curtain to expose the true power behind Rome —

much like Toto's pulling back of the curtain to expose "the great and powerful Wizard of Oz." Through its apocalyptic journeys Revelation offered a way of seeing —God's vision of hope for the world—as an alternative to Rome's violence and power.

The most spectacular of Revelation's apocalyptic journeys is chapter 12, the war in heaven and the dramatic rescue of the heavenly woman. John takes us to heaven to show us that the power behind Rome is Satan—and that Satan has already been defeated and thrown out of heaven. So Rome's imperial power on earth is only temporary, John assures us. It will last only until Satan can be tied up and thrown into the Abyss. Revelation 12 is a spectacular vision, complete with dragons and shape-shifting animals, a personified figure of "Earth" who rescues the mythic woman, and a heavenly chorus. The vision's message, presented by the chorus as in so many of Revelation's visions, proclaims: *"Now the salvation and power and the kingdom of our God and the authority of his Christ have come."* We are told to ally ourselves with the reign of God and Jesus, not with Rome or any other empire.

PROPHECY IS A TIMELY WARNING, NOT A PREDICTION

Revelation is an apocalypse; it is also prophecy. "Blessed is the one who reads aloud the words of the prophecy and blessed are those who hear," declares the third verse of the book (Rev 1:3). Prophecy is God's word of salvation and justice for the world.

The word "prophecy" holds great importance for Revelation, and also for dispensationalists. Indeed, it is their favorite word. "Twenty-eight percent of the Bible is prophecy," Tim LaHaye likes to tell his readers. But what does prophecy mean? We must discard our popular understanding of the word, as with the word "apocalypse," to understand the biblical meaning of prophecy.

Prophecy does not mean prediction of the future. The Bible is not like a horoscope, giving specific predictions for the future. A cartoon a few years ago featured a man reading the book *The Bible Code*, telling his wife, "Honey, guess what we're going to have for breakfast tomorrow?" In some people's minds the Bible is that kind of prophetic script or code, predicting future world events in detail—events as specific as the rise and fall of leaders in the Middle East and nations joining the European Common Market.

In the past fifty years a huge industry has sprung up around Christian prophecy, fueled especially by Israel's statehood in 1948 and its capture of the West Bank and East Jerusalem's holy sites in 1967. Hal Lindsey and the authors of the *Left Behind* novels read Revelation's prophecies in this way, as if they were predictions issued two thousand years ago about events that would happen in our century in Europe, in Israel, and the Middle East.

But predicting the future is not the biblical meaning of prophecy, in either the Christian or Jewish tradition. When Revelation calls itself prophecy it is situating its message in line with other biblical prophets like Jeremiah and Isaiah. Those prophets' task was to speak God's word—a word of salvation and justice for God's people and for the world. Their task was to set God's vision before the people so they could see it and live it. Prophets condemn injustice and greed; they advocate for the poor, for widows, and orphans.

When biblical prophets preached destruction, the purpose of their threats was almost always to warn of the consequences of destructive behavior, not to furnish play-by-play information about events in the future. The prophet's goal is to wake people up and turn people's hearts to God's vision of justice and generosity for the world. The future is not yet determined. There is hope that judgment can be averted.

As Jewish theologian Yehezkel Landau underscored in his 1983 critique of Ronald Reagan's Armageddon-focused view of the Bible, "biblical prophecy is not a foretelling of inevitable doom or destruction. Rather, it is a timely warning combined with a promise." In the Bible, the prophetic outcome is "always conditional," Landau explains, "for it is dependent on human behavior in response to God's word."[4]

A classic example of such a biblical prophet is Jonah. When Jonah finally agreed to journey to Nineveh he preached the message that God had given him: "In just forty days this great city will be destroyed" (Jon 3:4). This certainly sounds like a prediction, even specifying a date—forty days—for Nineveh's destruction. But the people of Nineveh listened to Jonah's word of prophecy. They turned to God, putting off their unjust ways. God saw their change of heart and God relented. God did not destroy the city of Nineveh as threatened. Forty days passed and no destruction happened.

Does that mean that Jonah was a false prophet, since his predicted destruction did not happen? According to the logic of the dispensationalist definition of prophecy, we would have to conclude that either Jonah was a false prophet or that his words were not prophecy, since his prediction did not come to pass. Jonah himself was angry that God did not carry through on what Jonah saw as a predetermined forty-day script for Nineveh's future. But biblical prophecy does not give a predetermined timetable for world events. God does not follow a script.

The book of Revelation, with its predictive-sounding threats, was written to function in a way similar to Jonah's "timely warning" to Nineveh that "In just forty days this great city will be destroyed." While Revelation's prophetic threats sound concrete, their primary purpose is to warn people. Revelation does not map out a divine script for the world's destruction. The goal of prophecy is rather to turn the world to God, to lift up a vision, so that threats of destruction will not be carried out. God does not want to hurt or destroy the world, and God certainly does not determine the script in advance.

Like the visionary journeys in Dickens's *A Christmas Carol*, Revelation's visions of seals, trumpets, bowls, and other manifestations are meant to be a wake-up call. They unveil the urgency of God's justice and judgment by taking us on terrifying journeys, all with the goal of persuading us to ally ourselves with God's vision for our world. The journeys are not intended as literal predictions of events that *must* happen; they are nightmarish warnings of what *may* happen—if we do not follow God's nonviolent Lamb.

The trumpets of Revelation, for example, are modeled on trumpet passages from the Old Testament such as those in Ezekiel chapter 33. Ezekiel's prophetic role was as a sentinel who "blows the trumpet and warns people," so that the "wicked turn from their ways and live; turn back, turn back from your evil ways." If Revelation's trumpets follow the model of Ezekiel's, then their purpose is also warning—to exhort people to "turn back and live." The trumpets of both Revelation and Ezekiel serve notice to oppressors about the consequences of their evil ways. Their aim is to turn people to God, not to issue predictions. Exhortation is the function of Revelation's other visions as well, as Harvard professor Elisabeth Schüssler Fiorenza has convincingly argued.[5]

Revelation is written in intimate conversation with the Old Testament, with more than one thousand allusions to the Hebrew scriptures, by some counts. Revelation employs various beasts and abominations from the book of Daniel as well as extensive imagery from Isaiah, Jeremiah, and Ezekiel. Dispensationalists claim that Revelation was written to furnish the detailed chronology of Daniel's seventieth week, but there is no justification for this assertion. Revelation does not offer a play-by-play predictive script, and certainly does not spell out in advance the events of the final seven years of life and death on earth.

God cannot be emprisoned in a predetermined script. This is perhaps the most dangerous aspect of the dispensationalist view of prophecy. This view of God and history leads to appalling theology and ethics. Rayford Steele, *Left Behind*'s hero, is given multiple opportunities to thwart or destroy the evil Antichrist early in the series. But he refrains from doing so because he views the Bible as a preset script dictating that the Antichrist "must" live for seven more years. "The Scriptures are clear that the Antichrist will not meet his demise until a little over a year from now."[6] And again, "the Bible foretold that Antichrist would then be resurrected and indwelt by Satan" for three and a half more years.[7]

Do the Scriptures really determine that millions more of the world's people must die, because God has a predetermined script that keeps the Antichrist alive for seven years? Can God not relent and change, as God did for Nineveh?

Dispensationalist theology espouses a deterministic view of prophecy, bordering on complacency. For them, biblical prophecy is "history written in advance," in very specific detail. "God has seen fit to forecast the future," LaHaye writes in *The Merciful God of Prophecy*, "and everything always happens just the way he said it would." Events in the Middle East "must" unfold in a certain sequence so that Jesus can return, a perspective that governs dispensationalists' view of U.S. foreign policy in Israel and Palestine. But this understanding of prophecy is not biblical. It precludes God's mercy and grace that are ever new. It puts God in a box. At worst, it can even encourage people to try to hasten the scripted apocalyptic events themselves, with deadly consequences for our world.

Revelation provides criteria for determining true and false prophets, criteria that have nothing to do with forecasting the future. Revelation condemns a woman in one of the seven churches who falsely "calls herself a prophet." This "Jezebel" is labeled a false prophet because she does not teach the true word of God, not because her predictions do or do not come to pass—prediction is of no concern to the author of Revelation. She preaches a message that accommodates Roman culture, "she teaches and beguiles my servants to practice immorality and eat food sacrificed to idols" (Rev 2:20). John, by contrast, is a true prophet because he proclaims God's salvation and truth.

Still the future is on everyone's minds today. We frail humans have a real longing to know the future. Dispensationalism cultivates this longing and then claims to answer it by correlating world events to its end-times script on a daily basis. The online Prophecy Club at the Left Behind Web site offers tantalizing headlines like, "Now you can predict incredible events." It encourages readers to speculate how the next events in Israel, Iraq, and Europe "can be foretold by anyone who understands end-times prophecy."[8]

But according to the Bible, foretelling events and figuring out the future in detail is not God's will for us. When Jesus' disciples try to find out specifics about his return, Jesus tells them that it is "not for you to know the times and the seasons" (Acts 1:7; see also Matt 24:36). Only God—not even Jesus himself—knows the future.

Biblical prophecy tells us not the specifics about *what* the future holds, but *who* holds the future. We can know the most important thing about the future: God is the one who holds our future. We can know that God is faithful and keeps promises. But those promises are not scripted. We should not look to biblical prophecy for literal play-by-play predictions of future geopolitical events.

BEYOND "LITERALISM":
JOURNEYING MORE DEEPLY INTO REVELATION

How then should we read the book of Revelation? What does it say for us and for our world today, if not predictions of global events? Lindsey, LaHaye, and other dispensationalists claim to be reading the book of Revelation "literally," applying geopolitical predictions to today. But a literalist reading of Revelation is impossible, and they know it. Animals, angels, and other creatures appear in apocalypses in ways that defy a linear "this happens, then that happens" sequential reading. Apocalypses are visions, not reality TV.

In his *The Merciful God of Prophecy: His Loving Plan for You in the End Times*, LaHaye lays out the dispensationalist criteria for interpreting scripture literally: "When biblical writers intentionally use metaphors and symbols, we must try to understand what they meant to convey through these images. But when they speak plainly—when they employ nonpoetic language in a straightforward way—what right have we to pronounce their words 'metaphorical' or their ideas merely 'symbolic'?" In LaHaye's view, and the view of others who follow the dispensationalist line, most of the book of Revelation is "plain language" that must be interpreted literally.

But *The Late Great Planet Earth* and the *Left Behind* novels show how arbitrarily this criterion can be applied to Revelation. Given Revelation's highly visionary palette of imagery, the crucial question is what is literal or "plain language" and what is metaphorical, and who has the authority to decide.

Both LaHaye and Lindsey interpret the four horses of Revelation's chapter 6 symbolically, but then they insist on a literalistic reading of the white horse on which Jesus arrives for battle in chapter 19: "Jesus is going to appear from heaven on a horse. That's literal."[9] No basis is given for interpreting some horses literally, but not others. Revelation's "beasts" are not literal beasts, according to today's dispensationalists, but rather a "symbolic metaphor for the weapons employed by the Antichrist and his enemies"—which gives license to interpret them as nuclear weapons or any other military technology, real or imagined. Similarly, the moon only "looks like" it turns to blood in *Left Behind*—apparently not a literal image! Yet in the very same chapter LaHaye insists the world's seas and rivers must literally turn to blood and that a literal earthquake must simultaneously strike the whole world except Israel, defying geology. "An earthquake is coming, and it is not symbolic," LaHaye scolds "liberal" preachers and biblical scholars who refuse to take such imagery literally: "I ask you, is there anything difficult to understand about a passage that begins, 'Behold, there was a great earthquake'?"[10]

If earthquakes are literal for today's dispensationalists, other images are wildly symbolic—such as the woman clothed with the sun in Revelation 12.[11] Because the woman's appearance is described as a "wonder" or "sign," this allows Lindsey and LaHaye to recast her story in terms of high-tech twenty-first century military operations and narrow escapes into the ancient rock city of Petra in Jordan. The rabbi who serves as spiritual leader for the Tribulation Force lays out LaHaye's symbolic interpretation of Revelation 12: the "'woman' represented God's chosen people; the 'two wings,' land and air; 'her place,' Petra—the city of stone." Based on this interpretation, the Tribulation Force shuttles born-again Jews by helicopter to Petra in a new kind of exodus, evading armies of the Antichrist with gun battles to rival Indiana Jones's in Petra's narrow canyons. But did the author of Revelation really intend to prophesy military helicopters and airplanes when he wrote about the eagle's "two wings"? Who decides how such imagery should be interpreted? Fanciful symbolic interpretations involving helicopter gunships and directed-energy weapons range far afield of LaHaye's insistence on Revelation's plain language, and they belie his scathing critique of liberal preachers who interpret Revelation's earthquakes or other events in a nonliteral way.

A strictly literal interpretation of Revelation is neither possible nor desirable. The book's central image, after all, is a Lamb! Scholars debate many aspects of the historical Jesus, but no one argues that Jesus was a sheep. When Revelation pictures Jesus as a Lamb, this is a metaphor or symbol. John has wonderful reasons for depicting Jesus as a lamb—"Lamb" underscores Jesus' vulnerability and innocent suffering, and it links Jesus to the Passover lamb that saved the Israelites in the Exodus story. Picturing Jesus as a lamb resonates deeply for Christians, and indeed this image becomes key to Revelation's message for us today. But it is not an image you can take literally. Jesus was a human being, not a sheep. Revelation's imagery is deeper and more visionary than strict literalism allows.

Instead of trying to "figure out" Revelation's images literally, as if they were a code or script for the future, Revelation invites us to enter into its world of vision. The Greek word for what Revelation "shows" or "makes known" in the very first verse of the book is the same verb for "sign" as the signs in John's Gospel and in Revelation 12. This verse tells us that the whole book is intended not as a slavishly literal kind of showing, but a deeper sign-level. We are invited to go with John on the apocalyptic journey, to experience the book's transformative power. In order to go on that journey we have to let go of a literalist fixation, and come instead to Revelation with all our senses ready for God's voice. As Kathleen Norris argues in her commentary on Revelation, "this is a poet's book, which is probably the best argument for reclaiming it from fundamentalists. It doesn't tell, it shows, over and over again, its images unfolding, pushing hard against the limits of language and metaphor, engaging the listener in a tale that has the satisfying yet unsettling logic of a dream."[12]

Revelation is full of songs—heavenly choruses praising God and encouraging us to sing in the midst of tribulation. Just when the book begins to sound hopeless or despairing, a host of witnesses in heaven break into song. Even animals join the Lamb's chorus, singing along with a cacophony of "every creature in heaven and on earth and under the earth and in the sea." No other book of the Bible has shaped Christian hymns and music as much as Revelation, from Handel's "Hallelujah Chorus" to "When the Saints Go Marching In," to the "Battle Hymn of the Republic," African American spirituals, and even reggae ("Let's get together to fight this Holy Armageddon," from Bob Marley's "One Love"). Revelation's songs are not intended to be literalistic. Indeed, the metaphorical dimension is precisely what gives Revelation's songs their power. Songs connect us to something deeper: they evoke our capacity for solidarity and resistance, they give us hope.

Think of Revelation's imagery like that of a three-dimensional Magic Eye picture. The picture appears to be just flat rows of tiny, patterned shapes on the page. Only if you let go of a literalist fixation on each of those shapes and allow your eyes to blur does a deeper, three-dimensional picture come into view. My favorite Magic Eye is from the Shedd Aquarium in Chicago with the caption "Don't expect to see everything the first time." At first glance the picture looks like rows of blue and turquoise abstract shapes on a flat page. When you let go and blur your vision you suddenly begin to see the real picture: two dolphins jumping out of the water, and a whale diving down. A whole aquatic world comes to life inside the page, and you are drawn into this deeper world.

Revelation's world of vision is like that of a Magic Eye picture. It is an "Aha" kind of vision that draws us in to see the deeper picture. God invites us to let go of the flat page, to stop trying to figure out each literal detail of Revelation, and instead to enter further into the larger picture. As we read and meditate on the images of Revelation, we find whole new levels of God's vision for our world unveiled to us: We taste water that is not just water—it is living water, the river of life. We follow Jesus, the shepherding Lamb, who invites us to drink from springs of that living water. We hear God's lament for our world that is oppressed, and we witness the trial and judgment of oppressors in a suspense-filled courtroom. Finally, most wonderfully, we see God coming to earth to live with us in a beloved city—to wipe away all the world's tears.

SEEING THE BIBLE COMING TO LIFE

I am convinced that part of the reason the *Left Behind* novels and dispensationalist theology have such appeal today is that we Christians have not been passionate or urgent enough in telling our stories of those "Aha" moments of seeing God and the Lamb alive in the world. We have been too hesitant to share experiences of God's deeper picture coming to life in our lives.

In interviewing *Left Behind* readers for her book *The Rapture Culture: Left Behind in Evangelical America* Amy Johnson Frykholm heard the response over and over that the novels "bring the Bible to life." According to Frykholm, readers "attribute to *Left Behind* the bringing of these obscure images 'to life,' which often means bringing them into a scheme of logic, assimilating them into a cosmic story they can understand." The people she interviewed are hungry to see connections between the Bible and their life. The script of dispensationalism gives them a method for drawing those connections.

But the problem is that the dispensationalist method of drawing connections relies on a dangerous and false view of God and the Bible. The events where dispensationalists identify the Bible's cosmic plan coming to life are most of all world wars, bloody crashes, earthquakes, diseases, and other violent cataclysms. Disasters of sickening magnitude are welcomed by prophecy buffs because they evoke feelings that God is present and alive. "It's blood," Rayford says of the red-stained snow and burning hailstones falling all around him, "a sense of peace flooding his soul." With almost perverse joy, he welcomes bloody disasters as proof that "God is faithful."[13]

Similarly, as Rayford walks through his plane after overhearing the Antichrist's order to destroy San Francisco and Chicago he reflects on all the destruction. While he is disgusted by the violence, he nonetheless sees it all as the fulfillment of Scripture, and that comforts him:

On television he saw live reports from around the world. *Scripture had come to life. This was the Red Horse of the Apocalypse.* Next would come more death by famine and plagues until a quarter of the population of the earth that remained after the Rapture was wiped out. (LaHaye and Jenkins, *Nicolae*, 108; emphasis is the author's)

Rayford's view of Scripture coming to life in the destruction of San Francisco may appeal to thrill-seeking readers, but reflects an appalling view of God. Christians need to refute the notion that death and violence—"the Red Horse of the Apocalypse"—are where we see God most present and active in the world.

The Bible and the book of Revelation come to life most of all in life-giving experiences of hope, healing, and transformation. I have seen God in my life, and I believe that you have, too—not in the Red Horse of the Apocalypse, but in "Aha" moments of unexpected joy, in being embraced by what Jesus calls "abundant life." Revelation comes to life not in a predetermined script of violent disasters but rather in experiences of God's river flowing through your life, flooding you with a vision for God's healing of the whole world. God is not a script, God is love. It is in love—in the day-to-day miracles of our lives—that we meet God and that we see the Bible coming to life in our world.

South African pastor Allan Boesak experienced the book of Revelation coming to life in echoes of the Lamb's new song that he heard in the songs of black people struggling for freedom during the 1980s, when his country was in the grip of apartheid. The song to the Lamb in Revelation 5 anticipated the liberation that was coming to South African people:

> The song of the twenty-four elders is the same age-old song of Israel, and it vibrates with the same power and certainty . . . This is the kind of song oppressed people sing with zest and an almost unspeakable joy . . . "Worthy is the Lamb who was slain, to receive power and wealth and wisdom and might and honour and glory and blessing!"
>
> On a Sunday afternoon young black Christians pick up this ancient song and make of it a new song as they dance around a police vehicle just after a student has been arrested at our church service . . . The police, somewhat confused, somewhat bewildered, somewhat scared, release our friend. Others join us as we march, singing and dancing, back into the church. This is a new song, a

freedom song, and the power of it, the sheer joy of it, the amazing truth in it captivate and inspire thousands upon thousands throughout South Africa.

For although the seals of the scroll must still be opened, the scroll is not in the hands of Caesar but in the hands of the Lamb. And we will sing this new song until "every creature in heaven and on earth and under the earth and in the sea, and all therein," will say (5:13): "To the one who sits upon the throne and to the Lamb be blessing and honour and glory and might for ever and ever!" (Allan Boesak, *Comfort and Protest: The Apocalypse From a South African Perspective* [Philadelphia, Penn.: Westminster, 1987], 60–62)

The Bible comes to life for us in such concrete experiences— freedom songs that bring a prisoner's release in South Africa, or hope reborn for you in the midst of despair. The Bible comes to life in an "Aha" moment of insight, in the embrace of a community of forgiveness, in seeing the face of God in another person, in the scary but wonderful presence of the shepherding Lamb who leads you through even the toughest moments.

When God acts in the Bible, as Jesus announced, it is most of all to bring healing to outcasts, "recovery of sight to the blind . . . to set at liberty those who are oppressed," to share abundant life with us and restore us to joy. This is how the Bible comes to life in our world—not as a literalistic script for end-times violence and disasters but as a river of hope and life flowing through our world, touching our lives.

There is a moment in *Left Behind* when Rayford Steele enters into this deeper, nonliteral sight of Revelation's world of vision. Picking up his wife Irene's Bible, Rayford begins to read, starting at the end, with Revelation 22: "Let the one who is thirsty come; let the one who wishes take the water of life without cost." Rayford is deeply moved by this passage about the water of life: "It struck him that he was thirsty, soul thirsty. But what was the water of life?"

That is the question the book of Revelation sets out to answer for first-century Christians in Asia Minor and can answer also for us today: What is God's water of life for us and for our world? Revelation is a book for everyone who is "thirsty, soul thirsty." Just as Revelation does not give Rayford Steele a literal glass of water for his soul thirst, so Revelation does not give us literal predications for the future. Its message—and its soul-reviving water of life—are much deeper.

The Journey Begins

Rome's Worship of Victory

*L*EFT BEHIND'S RAYFORD STEELE SHOULD have looked back a few verses more in chapter 22 of Revelation. He would have discovered one of the most beautiful visions in all of scripture: a river of life-giving water, bright as crystal, flowing from the throne of God and of the Lamb. You and I can find that river, too.

A river runs through the whole Bible. Starting in Genesis, east of Eden, the river weaves through the Old and New Testaments to its culmination at the end of the Bible in the beautiful New Jerusalem vision of Revelation. The whole Bible tells the story of God's mystical river flowing out through the world and through people's lives, bringing life and healing to all that it touches. For soul-thirsty people who set out to rediscover God's presence in their lives, the path is along this river, back through the Bible. The source of the river, from which its life-giving power flows, according to Revelation, is a throne—the throne of God and of the Lamb, Jesus.

As we trace this river to its source and enter more deeply into the vision of God at the heart of Revelation, we should first step back into the ancient world in which Revelation was written. Reading the book of Revelation or any biblical book is like discovering a cache of old letters in your attic. You want to learn everything you can about the people who wrote and read those letters so long ago. Why are their letters so passionate? What was the urgency? When you read Revelation you are reading someone else's mail—letters written originally by John of Patmos with an urgent message for churches in Asia Minor almost 2000 years ago. These letters tell a fascinating story that still speaks to us today.

Come with me on a journey back to the ancient Roman province of Asia, to a time just before the turn of the first century (around 96 A.D.). This is a journey back through the streets and cities of what is now western Turkey, along the blue waters of the Aegean Sea, a journey rich in visual imagery and archeology. This journey takes us through some of the grandest cities of the Roman Empire, the cities for which Revelation was written: Ephesus, Pergamon, Smyrna.

As we sail into their majestic harbors or walk through the gates of these ancient cities and down their streets, everywhere we turn we see triumphal monuments and buildings made of gleaming white marble. These monuments celebrate Roman gods and leaders. Most importantly, these monuments celebrate the military victories of mighty Rome.

ROME'S VISION OF VICTORY: *NIKE*

Romans celebrated Victory, but more than that—they *worshiped* Victory. This is key to grasping the urgency of Revelation, for John wrote Revelation in opposition to the empire's entire ideology and worship of Victory. The Roman goddess of military victory was named *Victoria* in Latin, or *Nike* in Greek. Portrayed as a winged goddess, she is the inspiration for the wing-like symbol on running shoes today.

Victory personified was emblazoned everywhere in the Roman Empire. Soldiers carried images of Victory into battle on their flags and trophies. Senators burned incense to Victory as they entered the Roman senate building.[1] Cities erected statues of Victory—or Nike—with her foot on the globe, symbolizing Rome's conquest of the whole world. Coins portrayed her standing beside the emperor, reminding anyone who handled money of Rome's military success.

A whole series of Roman Victory coins minted in the year 71 A.D., for example, in celebration of Rome's victory in the Jewish Revolt, depict the goddess Victory "setting up a trophy over a prostrate Jew . . . Victory crowning [Emperor] Vespasian, as he sacrifices in front of an arch."[2] The message was clear and strong: Rome's Victory—or Nike—in wars was what made peace and prosperity possible. No one ought to dare to oppose Rome's dominance over the world. Even a homemade graffiti inscription scrawled on a rock in rural Arabia at the end of the first century shows the widespread acceptance of this fact: "Romans always win."[3]

But John, writing only one generation after Rome's brutal crushing of the Jewish Revolt, was a prophet who dared to declare that Romans do *not* always win. John dared to oppose Rome's dominance and Victory with the vision of the victory of God's Lamb, Jesus. In his apocalypse John characterized Roman power and conquest not as the goddess Victory but as a demonic whore riding on a multiheaded beast, greedily seducing and destroying the entire world. John labels the entire Roman economy, including the widespread slave trade as "fornication."[4] Indeed, his apocalypse gives one of the most scathing critiques of the Roman Empire ever written by anyone in the ancient world.

The Roman Empire was still glorying in its victory over the Jewish Revolt at the time John was writing. Earlier victory processions had included elaborate battle reenactments, complete with Jewish captives paraded through the streets with their hands bound behind their backs. These parades were more than just ticker-tape victory celebrations. They were meant to send a message to people everywhere that any attempt at resistance to Rome would be punished. At the culmination of the victory parade in the city of Rome, thousands of Jewish captives were executed while the rest were sold as slaves.

The story of that victory procession in Rome after the Jewish Revolt is preserved in marble reliefs on the Arch of Titus, an imperial monument erected in 81 A.D. A closer look at the arch's imagery can help us understand Rome's theology of Victory, the very theology that the book of Revelation opposes. On one side, under the archway we see carved scenes of conquest—the golden menorah captured from Jerusalem's Temple, along with other booty, being carried off in triumph, followed by Jewish captives with their hands bound. The other side of the arch portrays the victorious imperial mythology: Emperor Titus riding in a chariot driven by the goddess Roma, while the goddess Victory crowns his head with a triumphal wreath. Around the arch are more images of Nike—or Victory. The arch's spandrels are "filled with flying Victories with their feet on globes, carrying Roman banners, trophies, laurel wreaths and palm branches."[5]

Imagine you are a Christian living in a world "filled with flying Victories . . . carrying Roman banners." John never traveled to Rome to see the Arch of Titus, but as far away as Asia Minor he and the people of his churches were confronted daily with the image of Rome's flying Victory goddess on monuments and altars in their own cities. The picture of these flying Victory or Nike figures is not so different from John's description of the flying messenger in chapter 14 of Revelation: "Then I saw another angel flying in midheaven with an eternal gospel to proclaim to those who dwell on earth . . . saying with a loud voice, 'Fear God . . . and worship the One who made heaven and earth.'"

Is it too far-fetched to imagine that the Revelation's flying messenger might be intended as a deliberate challenge to Roman flying Victory goddesses announcing another military victory? The message or "eternal gospel" that Revelation's flying messenger proclaims is the opposite of Rome's. It is the proclamation that the ultimate glory and Victory belong to God, not to Rome or to any empire. This message is confirmed by a second flying messenger following close behind, bearing the message of Rome's demise, "Fallen, fallen is Babylon the great!"

To understand the radical nature of Revelation's counter-theology of victory, we must underscore that the Roman Empire's own theology of military victory or *nike* would have been known by everyone in Revelation's churches. People saw Nike proclaimed whenever they walked down the street or used a coin to shop in the market.[6] Imperial slogans like Julius Caesar's "I came, I saw, I conquered" trumpeted Rome's political invincibility. Lest Rome's subjects fail to comprehend the message of military conquest and Victory, Rome even minted *capta* coins after each war that depicted the defeated province as a captive prisoner being stepped on by Roman generals. Familiarity with Rome's vision of Victory, or Nike, would have been as much a part of the culture of Revelation's cities as the pervasive Nike imagery and corporate identity is in our culture today. In antiquity as in our own day, the Nike symbol sent a message of global dominance and power to which any resistance was futile.

John wrote the book of Revelation in order to lift up the vision of Jesus as a counter-message to the empire's theology of Victory, or Nike. The book of Revelation deals with the opposition between two kinds of power in our lives and in our world: the power of oppressive systems of domination versus the power of God's Lamb to bring life and healing.[7] This is the starting point of Revelation's theology, the point on which John stakes his strongest claim. In place of the vision of military Victory and power offered by Rome—a vision still offered by imperial powers today—Revelation offers the amazing vision of the victory of God's slain Lamb, Jesus.

Lamb Power

JESUS IS THE MAIN CHARACTER in Revelation. The book's
opening line tells us that it is an "apocalypse of Jesus Christ."
Revelation's primary purpose is to tell us the story of Jesus, not to
predict end-times events in Europe or the Middle East.[1] And who is
Jesus? Jesus is first presented in the book as a majestic, human-like
figure with the sword in his mouth. But this depiction is quickly
eclipsed by the portrayal of Jesus as a Lamb. As New Testament
scholar David Barr notes, "Once introduced, the Lamb dominates
the rest of the action. It is the Lamb who gathers the 144,000 holy
warriors on Mt. Zion (Rev 14:1); it is the Lamb on whom the
armies of evil make war (Rev 17:14); it is even the Lamb who mar-
ries and rules after the war (Rev 19:7, 22:3)."[2]

The Lamb is an amazing and yet wonderfully disarming vision.
In the face of Rome's ideology of Victory, the victorious Lamb of
Revelation looks almost incongruous. In place of overwhelming
military strength, we are given the image of the Lamb's nonviolent
power. In place of Rome's image of inflicting slaughter on the
world, Revelation tells the story of the Lamb who has been slaughtered—and who still bears the scars of that slaughter. This reversal

of images must have come as a big surprise to first-century Christians accustomed as they were to Rome's images of power and victory. Revelation undertakes to reveal what true power and true victory is: At the heart of the power of the universe stands Jesus, God's slain Lamb.

We first meet Jesus as the Lamb quite unexpectedly in chapter 5 of Revelation, in the heavenly vision that follows the seven opening letters of chapters 2 and 3. In keeping with the apocalyptic pattern of Revelation, the book takes us on a journey behind the veil into heaven itself where we see God seated on a beautiful throne. All creation is singing praise to God. Singing and worship are central to Revelation, a fact often overlooked by people who see the book only as a system of end-times predictions and timetables. In Revelation we sing our way into God's new vision for our world, more than in any other book of the Bible.

Seated on the throne in heaven, God holds a scroll sealed shut with seven seals that must be opened. But who is worthy to open this scroll? God's voice from the throne tells John in chapter 5, "Do not weep, for the lion of the tribe of Judah, the Root of David, has conquered so that he can open the scroll and its seven seals." Two words in this admonition—"lion" and "conquer" (*nike* in Greek)— lead us to expect that a fierce animal will appear to open the scroll with its claws, like the conquering lions in gladiatorial spectacles. A lion would be typical for an apocalypse; such fierce animals are often introduced to advance the plot. In Second Esdras, for example, the Messiah is portrayed as a roaring lion prophesying judgment against the Roman eagle and its violence.[3]

But Revelation pulls an amazing surprise. In place of the lion that we expect, comes a Lamb: "Then I saw between the throne and the four living creatures and among the elders a Lamb standing as if it had been slaughtered" (Rev 5:6). It is a complete reversal. Actually the Greek word John uses is not just "lamb," but the diminutive form, a word like "lambkin," "lamby," or "little lamb" (*arnion* in Greek)—"Fluffy," as Pastor Daniel Erlander calls it.[4] The only other place this word *arnion* is used in the New Testament is where Jesus says he is sending his disciples out into the world "as lambs among wolves" (Luke 10:3). No other apocalypse ever pictures the divine hero as a Lamb—Revelation is unique among apocalyptic writings in this image.[5] The depiction of Jesus as a Lamb shows him in the most vulnerable way possible, as a victim who is slaughtered but standing—that is, crucified but risen to life.

Reminiscent of the servant-lamb of Isaiah 53, who "is led to the slaughter, and like a sheep to the shearer is silent," the Lamb of Revelation became the victor not by militaristic power and slaughter but rather by *being slaughtered*. From beginning to end, Revelation's vision of the Lamb teaches a "theology of the cross," of God's power made manifest in weakness, similar to Paul's theology of the cross in First Corinthians. Lamb theology is the whole message of Revelation. Evil is defeated not by overwhelming force or violence but by the Lamb's suffering love on the cross. The victim becomes the victor.

Lamb theology is what true victory or true *nike* is. For we, too, are "victors" or followers of the Lamb on whom the term *nike* or conquering is bestowed. This is one of the amazing features of the book. Much of Revelation can sound so violent, but we have to look at the subversive heart of the book—the redefinition of victory and "conquering"—to understand how Revelation *subverts violence itself*. Just like the Lamb, God's people are called to conquer not by fighting but by remaining faithful, by testifying to God's victory in self-giving love. This subversive power of Lamb theology throughout the book of Revelation is what *Left Behind* and the dispensationalists completely miss.

Key to understanding our role as followers of the Lamb and his way of life is chapter 14, the picture of the 144,000 people who "follow the Lamb wherever he leads."[6] If we can resist getting fixed on the number 144,000, and instead go deeper into the scene, we find a marvelous picture of the Christian community. In the view of Chilean scholar Pablo Richard, Revelation 14 is the central scene for the entire book that gives a picture of our life as the people of God on earth.[7] The Christian community is portrayed as "those who follow the Lamb." Our calling as Christians is simply to be followers of the Lamb, standing with him, going wherever he leads.

Revelation wants us to see that we "have the Lamb's power in us," writes Methodist pastor Christina Le Moignan.[8] Her book cover shows a lamb standing in the middle of a shopping mall. The Lamb is an image Revelation wants us to carry with us into our lives, like the children's nursery rhyme "Mary had a little lamb"— Wherever we go, to school, to work, or shopping, everywhere in the world, the lamb is with us, leading us into a new way of life.

"Lamb power" is what Ward Ewing calls Revelation's new way of life, a lifestyle oriented around Jesus' self-giving love. "Lamb power is the power of vulnerable but strong love to change the world," he writes.[9] It is the power of nonviolent resistance and courage in opposition to injustice; it is the power of solidarity and forgiveness. "In all things, large and small, personal and political, the power of vulnerable love can bring healing." We constantly must choose between the way of the Lamb and the way of the beast. Living by Lamb power means we accept the cross as the ultimate expression of love. For Ewing, the apocalyptic events of September 11, 2001, that took place only a few blocks away from the Episcopal Seminary in New York where he is president, have convinced him all the more of the necessity of Lamb power. "If we are to follow the Lamb, we cannot remain safe and secure . . . Vulnerability—the primary characteristic of Lamb power—includes by definition the possibility of suffering."[10] Lamb power is the power of our acts of hope and resistance, our songs and solidarity, to overcome the terror of the beast.

At the very heart of God is a slain Lamb—Jesus, Revelation tells us. And the key to the book is that this slain Lamb has somehow "conquered."

CHAPTER

7

Nonviolence

Conquering in Revelation

AS DISCUSSED IN CHAPTER 5, one theme that runs through the entire book of Revelation is the theme of victory. The book's word for "victory" is the Greek verb *nikan*, the same word used in Roman imperial theology of *Nike*—a word that can be translated in English as either "victory" or "conquering." In Revelation, both Jesus and the evil beasts claim to be "victors" who "conquer." As the book unfolds, the heart of Revelation's story is the opposition between two kinds of victory, the beast's and the Lamb's. Christians must make a choice between these two.

As followers of the Lamb, Christians take part in the conflict with the beast and share in the Lamb's victory. The theme of victory or conquering unites the various sections of Revelation, from the promises to the victor in the seven opening letters to the final New Jerusalem vision of Revelation 21–22. The question is how our victory takes shape in the middle section, as the conflict of Revelation unfolds and the world becomes the arena for the struggle between two very different models of conquering.

Does our victory involve armed combat and war, like the helicopters and guns of *Left Behind*'s Tribulation Force and Hal Lindsey's battle scenarios? Or is it a spiritual victory? Or something else
all together? These are crucial questions for us as we seek to understand Revelation's message in our world of violence today. I asked
these questions in a Bible study group of Latinos and Anglos at the
People's Seminary in Burlington, Washington, in the spring of
2003. We had just listened to a radio interview enlisting the book
of Revelation as support for war in Iraq. True, the interviewee
acknowledged, Jesus preached a gospel of peace, but in his view
the gospels' portrait of a peaceful Jesus is trumped by the more
violent Jesus of Revelation: "The same suffering Messiah is also in
the book of Revelation going to be the conquering Messiah," the
man declared. "Just read Revelation." But was he right? Together,
we wanted to read Revelation and discover for ourselves how Revelation understands our role as followers of the "conquering Messiah," Jesus.

We looked up each of the references to "conquering" or "victory" (the Greek word *nikan*) in Revelation in a concordance, like a
detective conducting an investigation. You can do this exercise, too.
The term is used sixteen times in Revelation, more than half of all
the occurrences of the word in the entire New Testament. What
we found as a result of our investigation is that Revelation delin-
eates two very different models of conquering: the beast's model
and the Lamb's model—and that this difference defines our role.

The theme of "conquer" or "victory" begins in chapters 2 and 3 of
Revelation, with the seven opening letters to the seven churches. The
letters are also the place where we learn important information about
the real-world situation of the churches to which John is writing in
Ephesus, Smyrna, Pergamon, and other ancient cities. Each letter follows the same overall pattern of describing the church's strengths and

weaknesses, then calling for repentance and giving a wonderful promise. Each letter's promise names the followers of Jesus as "victors" (literally "the one who conquers"—the Greek verb, *nikan*), the same word for the Rome's goddess of Victory.

John's labeling of God's people as "victors" or "conquerors" right from the outset of the book, using such a politically loaded term, sets up the book's program of challenging Rome's imperial theology of victory or *nike*. "To the victor I will give to eat of the fruit of the tree of life that is in the paradise of God," the letter to Ephesus promises. Six more promises of future blessing are given to "the victor" in Revelation's opening letters to the churches—I will give hidden manna, a new name, white garments, citizenship (the status of "pillar") in God's New Jerusalem, the city that comes down from heaven. All of Revelation's seven letters include these promises to the "victor"—that is, they make promises to us. These promises will come to fulfillment for us in the final vision of New Jerusalem, at the end of the book, where the "victors" receive their inheritance.

The appearance of Jesus as a slain Lamb rather than the lion in chapter 5 of Revelation gives us the first and most important image for God's model of conquering, the image of Lamb power. But Revelation also knows all too well Rome's imperial model of conquering, a model very different from Jesus'. In the vision of the seven seals in Revelation 6, this model is represented by the four powerful horses of Roman power—conquest, war, famine, and death. Each of the horses reveals a different and terrifying aspect of Rome, with special attention to the economic injustice unveiled by the third horse. The first horse brings victory or "conquering" (*nikan*), a term repeated twice for emphasis:

> Then I saw the Lamb open one of the seven seals, and I heard one
> of the four living creatures call out, as with a voice of thunder,

"Come!" I looked, and there was a white horse! Its rider had a bow;
a crown was given to him, and he came out conquering and to conquer. (Rev 6:1–2)

The beasts of chapters 11 and 13, who also represent Rome,
inflict a similar violent conquering. They "make war and conquer
and kill" God's two witnesses, leaving their dead bodies to lie in the
street.

So does that mean that our own "conquering" will also involve
making war and killing? No, because chapter 12 describes a very
different model for God's people: "They have conquered him
(Satan) by the blood of the Lamb and by the word of their testimony, for they did not cling to life even in the face of death."

This verse, Revelation 12:11, is crucial for determining our role
in Revelation's entire argument. Previously in a mythic scene of
war in heaven, Satan was thrown out of heaven through the victory of Jesus' death and resurrection (See Jesus' similar description in
the Gospel of Luke, "I saw Satan fall like lightning"). In anger Satan
now goes off to try to make war on God's other followers on
earth—that is, he makes war on us. The presence of evil in our
world is due to Satan's temporary presence on earth, Revelation
explains, using highly mythic imagery. We live in the time between
his expulsion from heaven and the time when he is thrown into the
abyss in chapter 20.

God's people are to conquer Satan in two ways, Revelation tells
us, "by the blood of the Lamb and by the word of their testimony."
Because this verse is so central, we must look at each part in turn
to see how Revelation intends for us to be victors.

The first way God's people conquer is "by the blood of the
Lamb." Blood is a strong theme in Revelation, a fact that *Left Behind*
and Hal Lindsey's works capitalize on with an almost ghoulish fix-

ation. The fourth *Left Behind* novel, *Soul Harvest*, for example, closes with the image of hail turning to blood (based on Rev 8:7) and a readiness to welcome God's war: "Following God's shower of hail, fire, and blood, remaining skeptics were few. There was no longer any ambiguity about the war."[1]

But do Revelation's blood and the blood of the Lamb really prove the unambiguous necessity of war and bloodshed, as *Left Behind* claims? Not if we take the Lamb as our model. If the slain Lamb is our model it means that the blood of Revelation is first of all the *Lamb's own blood*, shed for us and for the world. Even the blood on Jesus' garments in Revelation 19 must be presumed to be his *own* blood, not anyone else's.

To follow the model of Jesus means that we conquer not by attacking anyone or shedding others' blood—but rather by identifying with Jesus' own blood that was shed when he was crucified by the Romans. This point has been convincingly argued by some of the great advocates of peace who have written on Revelation—Mennonite theologian John Howard Yoder[2] and most recently Lee Griffith in his *The War on Terrorism and the Terror of God*—and it is supported by the best New Testament scholars on Revelation. While "Revelation has acquired the reputation of being a book of considerable blood and terror," Griffith argues, this reputation "may not be so well deserved." Revelation does not advocate the use of violence or bloodshed. Revelation is more a book about terror *defeated* than terror inflicted, "which is why worship and liturgy are such a central feature of the book."[3]

The second way that God's people "conquer" Satan in Revelation 12:11 is by giving our word of testimony and being willing even to give our lives. Testimony or witness (the Greek word *martyria*) has amazing power both for Jesus and for us in the book of Revelation. The term comes from a courtroom context. The idea is that we conquer by putting the unjust empire on trial and telling the truth about it. The story of the two witnesses in chapter 11 shows the power of testimony, as does Jesus' own testimony (Rev 1:2). Chilean scholar Pablo Richard draws an analogy to the power of testimony in oppressive contexts today: "In Revelation, testimony always has a power to change history, both in heaven and on earth . . . John believes that the faith of the holy ones is what is going to make the empire tremble."[4] Indeed, Revelation aims to convince us that Jesus' model of Lamb power is a model of victory more powerful than Rome's model of *nike* as military conquering.

Revelation's first-century readers knew first-hand Rome's conquering power over the whole world. They were its victims. We, too, live in a world in which terror makes us feel powerless and we wonder how God can be victorious over evil. The "beasts" of the Roman Empire are long gone, but today's "beasts" of violence, economic vulnerability, global injustice, and other threats still stalk our world, causing almost irrational fear. In a post-September 11 world we need to testify to the wonder-working power of God's slain Lamb today more than ever. Revelation's message is that the beasts and their conquering do not have the last word. In chapter 15, "those who have conquered" the beast—that is, we ourselves—are pictured standing in heaven with harps of God in our hands, singing the song of Moses and the song of the Lamb.

VIOLENCE AND THE ARMIES OF HEAVEN?

The question of violence is of crucial importance as we evaluate Revelation's message for today. Throughout the middle chapters of Revelation, the words "conquering" and "make war" appear in close association, fueling the sense that the book is pro-war. There is no question that the book is full of conflict. But even in terms of the words themselves, there is a crucial difference between the words "conquer" and "make war" in Revelation. Evil rulers "make war" on the Lamb one final time in Revelation 17:14, but the Lamb "conquers" them—a typical use of the two words.

As I have suggested, Revelation carefully redefines the word "conquer" to make clear that the Lamb and his followers conquer only by their testimony and faithfulness—not by making war or killing. War is something done *against* God's people by evil beasts and by Rome, not something that God's saints or the Lamb practice in this book. Two verses of Revelation do indeed refer to Jesus as "making war"—Revelation 2:16 and 19:11—but the *way* he makes war is crucial. Jesus makes war not with a sword of battle but "by the sword of his mouth." The word is Jesus' only weapon— this is a reversal as unexpected as the substitution of a lamb for a lion. These reversals undercut violence by emphasizing Jesus' testimony and the word of God.

Moreover, there is no reason for thinking that any Christians take part in the war in Revelation 19. While dispensationalists make the claim that raptured saints are part of the "army of heaven" that returns to earth with Jesus to fight in Revelation 19:14 in what they call the "Glorious Appearing," this claim is not substantiated in Revelation. The fact that the army is said to be clothed in white linen does not make it equivalent to Christians, as Hal Lindsey and others try to argue on the basis of Revelation 19:8.[5] It is clearly identified as a heavenly army—and amazingly, no actual attack or war is ever pictured. The war is over as soon as it begins. This is because the victory has already been won in Jesus' crucifixion—and is not to be fought in a final cataclysmic war.

Thus, the message of the book of Revelation becomes a reframing of the whole concept of victory, giving victory first to the Lamb and then to us. Nowhere in Revelation do God's people "wage war." What they do is "conquer" or "become victors" (the same word in Greek)—and they do that by the Lamb's own blood and by their courageous testimony, not through Armageddon or war. In contrast to Rome's theology that defined Victory as military conquest, Revelation develops a counter-theology of the non-violent victory (*nike*) of Jesus, God's slain Lamb, in which "evil is overcome by suffering love," not by superior power.[6]

David Barr argues convincingly that the narrative of Revelation "turns the popular American understanding of the Apocalypse on its head. For in the popular imagination, God conquers by power and the violence of holy war is justified." It is crucial to recall that at key points Revelation transforms or even subverts violent stories with the image of the Lamb:

> It is poor reading to overlook this inversion and to read as if the Lamb has not replaced the Lion in this story. Similar inversions occur at every point in the story—even in the climactic scene in which the heaven Warrior kills all his enemies, for his conquest is by means of a sword that comes from his mouth, not by the power of his arm. (Barr, "Toward an Ethical Reading of the Apocalypse," 361)

Because the central image of Revelation is the slain Lamb—not the Lion—"John's story stands firmly against violence and domination." For all its holy war imagery, Revelation does not promote war.

There is "wonder-working power in the blood of the Lamb," as the old gospel hymn reminds us—a power we need today more than ever. It is not the power of violence. Rather, the power that we find in Jesus' blood is "Lamb power": It is the wonder-working power of God's vulnerable, nonviolent love to change the world.

The Exodus Story
in Revelation

A SERIES OF HORRIBLE PLAGUES that appears in the middle chapters of Revelation is unquestionably the most difficult aspect of the book. These are favorite chapters for dispensationalists with their view that Revelation 6–19 furnishes the detailed playbook for the seventieth week of Daniel 9. End-times films and novels focus in ghoulish detail on the disasters unleashed by "the seven trumpets and seven bowls." Oceans turn to blood, fiery hailstones rain down on earth, and the world plunges into darkness and death. Millions of people are killed following multiple tortures so hideous that the victims long for death. In the dispensationalist script, God inflicts pain on humanity and the cosmos in unspeakable proportions.

As I have mentioned earlier, the story of the dreadful plagues does not serve as prediction of what is to come, but instead a frightening threat. Still, it is hard to understand why God threatens people with such violent and terrifying plagues.

I am convinced that the plot of the biblical Exodus story provides a way to understand the plagues of Revelation's seven trumpets and seven bowls. Think of Revelation as a retelling of Exodus. In that ancient story, God heard the cry of the people suffering as slaves in Egypt. God threatened Egypt with ten plagues designed both to show God's power and to persuade Pharaoh to let the people go free. Similarly, in the book of Revelation, God hears the people's cries and threatens new plagues against Rome's oppression as part of the overall goal of liberation from injustice.

In John's view, God's people were experiencing a new Exodus, "not in Egypt but in the heart of the Roman Empire," suggests Pablo Richard. If Revelation is a new Exodus, then Jesus is the new Moses, leading his followers out of captivity to death and into a new Promised Land of life and healing. Christians are called to "come out" of empire and injustice, just as the Israelites were called to come out of slavery in Egypt.

The entire book of Revelation is full of Exodus imagery, linking the Christian journey to the Israelites' journey out of Egypt. God's people are not called to undertake any violent action in the book of Revelation; the Exodus connection underscores that. Rather, as in Exodus, salvation comes only through God's action and the blood of the Lamb.

The Israelites sang a victory song after crossing the Red Sea in the Exodus story. Similarly, in Revelation, God's people join in singing a song in praise of their deliverance by God and the Lamb. Chapter 15 makes the link explicit between Moses and the Lamb:

> I saw what appeared to be a sea of glass mixed with fire, and those who had conquered the beast and its image, standing beside the sea of glass with harps of God in their hands. And they sing the song of Moses, the servant of God, and song of the Lamb. (Rev 15:2–3)

This idea, that the Exodus story is reenacted in Revelation, is a valuable tool for comprehending the terrible plagues of death and disaster. The plagues serve for the conversion of the oppressors and for the liberation of God's people. Like the plagues brought against Pharaoh in Exodus, the violence of the plagues threatened against Rome in Revelation is the violence of release and liberation, not vengeance or cruelty. As Pablo Richard describes, the aim of this "Exodus in the bosom of the Roman empire is the conversion of the oppressors and idolators and the liberation of the holy ones. Repeating the Exodus, God attempts to rein in the Roman empire's rush to destroy the world."[1]

Revelation's story of bloody oceans, giant hailstones, and ecological catastrophe is not a prediction to be taken literally. Especially in the descriptions of the plagues, we should avoid both the gloating triumphalism and the slavish literalism that characterizes so much of dispensationalist writing. The purpose of Revelation's terrifying description of suffering is to wake up the world to God's vision for life and repentance, to wake us up so the threatened events will *not* come to pass. God is not a cosmic destroyer.

Even Revelation's most deadly visions serve John's overall goal of conversion and repentance. This is clear in the sixth trumpet vision, one of the most horrific, in which 200 million horses massacre one-third of the world's population. Not even Tim LaHaye interprets those horses literally, although he does present the millions of deaths as foreordained by God. But Harvard Professor Elisabeth Schüssler Fiorenza points out that the verses immediately following this deathly plague chide the people for their lack of repentance, showing that the ultimate purpose is exhortation to repentance: The rest of humanity "did not repent of the works of their hands . . . nor did they repent of their murders or sorceries or their immorality or their thefts" (Rev 9:20–21).[2]

Like Moses threatening Pharaoh with plagues, this verse under-scores that the purpose of Revelation's vision was to bring about repentance, not inflict cruelty. Over and over, through Moses' terrible threats, God tried to get Pharaoh to change his mind:

> Then the Lord said to Moses, "Go to Pharaoh and say to him, 'Thus says the Lord, the God of the Hebrews: Let my people go, so that they may worship me. For if you refuse to let them go and still hold them, the hand of the Lord will strike with a deadly pestilence your livestock in the field: the horses, the donkeys, the camels, the herds, and the flocks.'" (Exod 9:1–3)

Revelation's threats are like those of the Exodus story—similar to today's nightmarish doomsday writers, who warn of the consequences of ecological or nuclear destruction, argues Schüssler Fiorenza. The goal of such horrific apocalyptic imagery is to "shock the audience" into changing their lives.[3]

A fascinating conversation between an angel and an altar provides another explanation for the plagues—the logic of natural consequences. Waters and springs are turned to blood in the third bowl plague. The angel explains this terrible pollution with a boomerang-like logic of punishment that can be relevant also to our world today:

> You are just, O Holy One . . . for you have judged these things; because they shed the blood of saints and prophets, you have given them blood to drink. It is what they deserve. (Rev 16:5–6)

The phrase translated "It is what they deserve" comes from the Greek word *axios,* for "axiomatic," or self-evident. Revelation's angel is saying that oppressors who commit acts of violence will eventually unleash destructive consequences against themselves: "Because they shed blood . . . you have given them blood to drink. *It is axiomatic.*" It is as if the angel is saying: See, it is inevitable! The talking altar responds in agreement, "Yes, O Lord God, the Almighty, your judgments are true and just."

So it is axiomatic that Babylon/Rome and other empires that make people suffer and die will be given a taste of their own deadly medicine, an inevitable cause and effect. Similarly today, if we continue to damage and "oppress" the environment and cause global warming, we will live with the deadly consequence of these destructive actions—it is self-evident and inevitable.

There is also a suggestion of penalty language in this pronouncement. God promises to put on trial the imperial oppressors in a divine courtroom. Roman oppressors will be called to account for their unjust actions; they will be sentenced and receive "what is their due."

Victims of injustice have a special window into these stories that affluent Christians cannot fathom. Like the plagues of Exodus, the stories of Revelation speak most clearly to people who struggle under oppression—to "God's little people," as South African Allan Boesak calls them. For the rich and comfortable, the plagues sound vengeful and terrifying. But to people suffering under oppression the plagues are good news because they herald the end of the oppression itself.

Writing from the grass-roots communities of Latin America where he ministers as a priest, Father Pablo Richard suggests that people's cries for justice today have their parallel in the cries of victims in Revelation who cry out against Roman oppression. He offers a provocative interpretation in which Revelation's plagues refer not simply to natural disasters but to the way the effects of oppression fall disproportionately on the poor:

> Cosmic agonies of this kind are not "natural" disasters but rather the direct consequences of the structure of domination and oppression: The poor die in floods because they are pushed out of safe places and forced to live alongside rivers; in earthquakes and hurricanes the poor lose their flimsy houses because they are poor and cannot build better ones; plagues, such as cholera and tuberculosis, fall primarily on the poor because they are malnourished . . . Hence the plagues of the trumpets and bowls in Revelation refer not to so-called "natural" disasters, but to the agonies of history that the empire itself causes and suffers; they are agonies of the beast caused by its very idolatry and lawlessness. Today the plagues of Revelation are rather the disastrous results of ecological destruction, the arms race, irrational consumerism, the idolatrous logic of the market, and the irrational use of technology and of natural resources. (Richard, *Apocalypse: A People's Commentary*, 85–86)

"ALAS"—NOT "WOE"—FOR THE EARTH

In addition to the Exodus story, several other theological considerations are also important for navigating the middle chapters of Revelation. The most important is that God does not curse the world, nor does God sentence the earth to destruction.

After the fourth trumpet, an eagle flies through the air crying out "Woe" with a loud voice: "Woe, woe, woe to the inhabitants of the earth, at the blasts of the other trumpets that the three angels are to blow!" (Rev 8:13). This is only one of the many declarations of woe in Revelation. These "woes" sound terrifying, coming as they do in the midst of the plagues. Dispensationalists use the "woe" verses to explain that God has sentenced the world to awful destruction.

But "woe" is not really a helpful translation for the Greek word. Its sense is rather one of lament—like a mourner keening in grief, wailing out repeated cries of "Oh, oh, oh" at the death of a loved one. Spanish Bibles simply translate the sound as "Ay, ay, ay." I would translate the word as, "Alas." The meaning of the Greek word *ouai* is first of all a cry of pain, like the word "ouch" in English. It can mean "woe," but it can also express deep lamentation or mourning, as in the laments of the merchants and kings over Rome in chapter 18, "Alas, Alas, Alas, for the great city!"—the same Greek word *ouai*.[4]

It is as if God is crying "ouch" or "alas" on behalf of the suffering world: "*Alas* for the inhabitants of the earth." It is a subtle but significant shift in direction because "Alas" conveys God's sympathy in a way that "woe" does not.

This is important because dispensationalists use Revelation's "woe" verses to argue that God has consigned the world to cataclysmic destruction. Their arguments contradict the overall message of Revelation. In the tradition of the Exodus story and the Exodus plagues, Revelation makes clear that God sympathizes, grieves, and laments over the world's pain, even while threatening plagues to bring about the world's liberation from injustice.

As we ponder the message of Revelation, especially its difficult middle sections, we must remember the overarching promise that God still loves the world and cries out for its liberation. In the slain Lamb Jesus, God shares our cries and comes to deliver us. God does not curse the world. God loves the world enough to weep and lament for it, and even to come to dwell in it with us. God will never leave the world behind!

SALVATION INTERLUDES

Interludes of salvation and heavenly worship are another way that Revelation tempers the horrific plagues of Revelation's middle chapters. The Exodus-inspired plagues of seals, trumpets, and bowls do not come in unrelenting sequences. There is a delay in each sequence after the first six elements, which heightens the sense of suspense and brings an important rest stop in the midst of the threats of disaster.

The first six seals are opened in rapid succession in chapter 6, unleashing the four deadly horses and other symbols of Rome's oppression. We expect that the seventh seal will continue the rhythm of horror. Instead, the book delivers an amazing surprise. In place of the seventh seal we get a beautiful vision of white-robed martyrs from all "nations, tribes, peoples and languages" waving palm branches and singing before the throne of God and the Lamb: "Salvation belongs to our God who is seated on the throne, and to the Lamb!" In a wonderful paradox, the Lamb himself becomes their shepherd, leading people to God's shelter and to springs of the water of life. Tenderly, God wipes away all our tears. This vision of Revelation 7 is a favorite for many Christians, read at funerals and on All Saints' Day.

Only after this interlude of comfort and salvation does the Lamb open the seventh and final seal, which brings a period of silence over the whole world. The salvation interlude of chapter 7 reminds us that at those moments when judgment threatens most to overpower us the Lamb still breaks into our world with God's unexpected grace and love. Other interludes of Revelation between the sixth and seventh trumpet and bowl are no less powerful. Throughout the book, such songs and declarations of salvation break out in heaven at some of the most difficult moments, sustaining our faith on earth. Vibrant connections between singing and hope are an element largely overlooked by dispensationalists with their ubiquitous timetables.

THE COURTROOM OF THE LAMB:
JUSTICE, FOR THOSE WHO CRY TO GOD

In our age of terror, Revelation shows us that there is another way to deal with terrorism and injustice other than war: it is the way of the lawcourt, of putting evildoers on trial for their war crimes and sentencing them to punishment before God's throne of justice. Recall David Barr's statement that Revelation turns the popular holy-war understanding of Revelation on its head. Chapter 18 is an example of that. In Revelation 18 the final defeat of Rome/Babylon happens not on a battlefield but in a courtroom. Revelation overturns holy war discourse with a class-action lawsuit in the divine courtroom, a trial scene as riveting as any TV courtroom drama.

People who cry out for justice in the world, who are oppressed by tyrants, need to know that there is a divine lawcourt or tribunal before which their case can be brought. "Mothers of the Disappeared" in El Salvador or Argentina, who stood with photos of their missing husbands or daughters in the Plaza de Mayo month after month, deserve to know that they will receive answers as to what happened to their loved ones. Victims who cry out for justice need to know that God still says, as in the Exodus story, "I have heard the cry of my people and I have come down to deliver them." They need to know that it is "just a little while" before God will judge and vindicate their blood against their oppressors, as the fifth seal vision narrates their cries. That vindication happens in Revelation 19:2, at the close of the lawsuit on behalf of Rome's victims.

In the class-action lawsuit the plaintiffs bring their plea for justice before God who judges on their behalf. The plaintiffs are the saints, representing all of Rome's victims who have been killed on earth. The defendant is Babylon/Rome and all other oppressive regimes throughout history.[5] The charge is murder: "In you was found the blood of prophets and of saints, and of all who have been slaughtered on earth" (Rev 18:24). The judge is God, who sentences Rome to receive a like measure of its own unjust medicine at the hands of its victims:

> Mix a double draught for her in the cup she mixed. As she glorified herself and lived luxuriously, so give her a like measure of torment and grief . . . for mighty is the Lord God who judges her. (Rev 18:6–8)

Since Rome is referred to as "her" and "she" in these verses, we need to say a word about the feminine characterization of the evil empire throughout chapters 17 and 18—especially since the personification of Rome as a garish whore wearing gold jewelry and a scarlet dress is one of the most unforgettable images of Revelation. In the history of art and literature, the whore of Babylon has become the ultimate "Jezebel" in most people's minds, personifying the "fatal attraction" of the powerful evil temptress who seduces her victims with her irresistible golden cup of fornications. Read literally, this image can fuel the worst misogynist fantasies—a reading we must resist. A literal reading also makes the punishment of the prostitute in Revelation 17:16 sound like a horrific scene of gang rape. Some of my female students have visceral reactions at the descriptions of the whore's torture, as well they should if it describes the literal torture scene of a woman's body.[6]

But we should not read the image of the whore of Babylon literally, just as we do not read the image of Jesus as a Lamb literally. Rome was an *empire*, not a woman. The Greek word for "city" is the feminine noun *polis*. In the ancient world it was conventional to personify cities as feminine figures, but this reflects only grammatical gender—not literal gender. The personification of Rome as a whore was much like what political cartoonists do today, representing the United States in the figure of the Statue of Liberty or Uncle Sam. What was so audacious for Revelation was to overturn Rome's self-image as the goddess Roma or Victory with the political cartoon of the empire as a whore.

The charge of "fornication" or "trafficking" against Babylon/ Rome has nothing to do with sex but is rather an economic charge— Rome lives by its predatory trade, trafficking in resources from the farthest points of the Roman Empire. Rome's wealth may also have been seductive for the very few wealthy or middle-class Christians who were striving to advance economically. What is highlighted throughout this entire scene is the economic and political critique of Rome, not a critique of women. The scene culminates in the three-fold laments of the kings, merchants, and mariners.

Joy breaks out in heaven and on earth when Rome's sentence is announced, with the post-trial celebration of plaintiffs extending even to the celebration of God's angels in heaven:

Rejoice over her, O heaven, you saints and apostles and prophets!
For God has given judgment for you against her. (Rev 18:20)

By contrast, Rome's rich merchants and kings weep over the loss of their wealth, wailing out their refrains of "Alas, alas, alas."

The message of the trial scene of Revelation 18 is that God desires justice in the divine courtroom. Revelation replaces the discourse of war with this final courtroom judgment against Rome and all other unjust empires. Those who oppress the world with their unjust economic structures and violence will be sentenced and punished, Revelation promises. Their empires will come to an end. In Jesus, the slain Lamb, the new reign of God has already begun to dawn.

In this climactic scene of chapter 18, Revelation calls on its audience to engage in the struggle for God's new world of salvation with justice. Using powerful Exodus language, the book calls on us to "come out" of empire and injustice so that we are not taking part in Babylon's/Rome's sins. We are to be followers of God's slain Lamb, Jesus, and to participate with him in God's new world. In every way, Revelation wants us to be grasped by a new and wonderful vision of Lamb power—the power of nonviolent love to change the world.

9

Hijacking the Lamb

Addiction to Wrath and War

To TELL THE STORY OF Revelation is to tell the story of
Jesus, the Lamb, and ultimately to tell the story of God—
since the Lamb is beside God throughout the entire book.

The slain Lamb's victory through suffering love is the heart of
the Revelation story. I want to say again that this theology, this
counter-understanding of victory in the Lamb, is more relevant
today than ever. In the face of terrorism and the glorification of
war, we need the vision of "Lamb power" to remind us that true
victory comes in our world not through military might but
through self-giving love. Revelation's conquering Messiah is the
slain but standing Lamb, the very opposite of Rome's victory
image. In Revelation, Jesus conquers not by inflicting violence but
by accepting the violence inflicted upon him in crucifixion.

Needless to say, dispensationalist Christians tell the story of the
Lamb very differently—as a vengeful war story, not a story of suffering love. We should be outraged that their war story is the version that Americans are exporting to the world in the name of

Christianity. That version, as in *Left Behind*, features a tough-guy Lamb who inflicts the "Wrath of the Lamb Earthquake" over the whole world (except Israel). For them, the heart of God is, first of all, this heart of wrath and terror against the world—the wrath of the Lamb—not a heart of suffering love on behalf of the world. Indeed, what my students who grew up in dispensationalist or fundamentalist homes remember most powerfully from their childhoods is the fear and threat of the wrath of God and the Lamb.

The phrase "the wrath of the Lamb," occurs only once in Revelation, in chapter 6 (Rev 6:16)—and then only on the lips of people who are trying to flee. In twenty-eight other references to the Lamb throughout the book of Revelation, *John never again refers to the Lamb as wrathful.* Yet "wrathful" is the favorite dispensationalist description for the Lamb. Most of the third *Left Behind* novel, *Soul Harvest*, describes the aftermath of the "Wrath of the Lamb Earthquake" with graphic descriptions of bleeding and decapitated bodies. This event becomes a central point of reference for the novel's timeframe— "Where were you during the Wrath of the Lamb Earthquake?"

By making wrath their dominant imagery for Christ, dispensationalists have betrayed the mission of the Lamb in Revelation. The *Left Behind* books skip over the Lamb's shepherding and sheltering action in Revelation 7—the Lamb who leads us to pasture in God and wipes our tears. Most regretably, they omit the river of life that flows from the throne of the Lamb in chapter 22. The *Left Behind* Lamb provides no comfort, no life. Instead of vulnerability or shepherding, their primary image of the Lamb becomes wrath and war.

We must make a choice as we read the story of the Lamb. To whom will we turn? To the violent, crusading Messiah, the wrath-filled "Terminator" Lamb of Tim LaHaye and John Hagee? That Lamb is like a muscled action figure whose Tribulation Force followers conduct paramilitary operations out of an underground bunker. To be sure, that version of the Lamb's story offers a certain way of "making Scripture come to life," and that has strong appeal for people. But what kind of life? Ultimately, that story is just another version of imperial Roman victory through military power. The Tribulation Force of *Left Behind*, and the rampaging armies of Hal Lindsey, win victory for the good guys with superior military power and God on their side. But their God does not look much different from the Roman generals who brought about victory through violent conquest.

The heart of our difference is this: dispensationalists do not seem to believe the Lamb has truly "conquered" or won the victory when he was slaughtered. They preach the saving power of the blood of the Lamb in Jesus' crucifixion, but it is not quite enough saving power for them. They need Christ to come back again with some real power, not as a Lamb but as a roaring lion. Jesus has to return so he can finish up the job of conquering. As Hagee puts it, "The first time He came to earth, Jesus was the Lamb of God, led in silence to the slaughter. The next time He comes, He will be the Lion of the tribe of Judah who will trample His enemies until their blood stains His garments, and He shall rule with a rod of iron. Even so, come Lord Jesus!"[1]

But there is no indication that the author of Revelation ever wants to call upon Jesus to return as a lion. John very deliberately replaces the lion with the Lamb in chapter 5 and never again refers to Jesus as a lion. Only evil figures are identified as lion-like in subsequent chapters of Revelation—the locusts have teeth like lions in chapter 9, and the horses of death have heads like lions.

So where do dispensationalists get the idea for Jesus to return as a lion? I say they fabricate this lion-like Jesus because they have a problem with the Lamb's weakness and vulnerability. They crave the avenging Jesus who will return as a lion and show his true power and fury: "This is no weak-wristed, smiling Jesus who comes to pay the earth a condolence call," Hagee says about Christ's future return. "This is a furious Christ, ready to confront the gathered armies of the world on a plain called Armageddon."[2]

VOYEURISM, ARMEGEDDON, AND THE ADDICTION TO WAR

Armageddon is the event that dispensationalists crave above all else—the "main event" as Lindsey describes it.[3] The word Armageddon appears only once in the entire book of Revelation (Rev 16:16), but dispensationalists make it the book's centerpiece. Armageddon will not just be a single battle, says LaHaye, but "actually consists of at least four 'campaigns' and spreads over almost all of the land of Palestine." The first campaign is to begin in Petra, or Edom, where the Lord "soils His clothing in the blood of His enemies."[4] Blood will flow so high that it will reach up to the horses' bridles in this war, as LaHaye likes to describe the battle of Armageddon. It will be a military spectacle of "shock and awe" on a scale never imagined.

Dispensationalists argue that their eagerness for Armageddon is only an eagerness for Jesus' return. Yet Jesus could return in *Left Behind* without so much violence and death. So what is the attraction of violence? Why are exaggerated blood and death so prominent in every dispensationalist version of the storyline?

The answer is the escapist Rapture of saints from the earth up to heaven. From high above the earth dispensationalists plan to watch the whole grand spectacle of earth's final war and destruction. The Rapture means that they will escape having to suffer any violence, yet will be able to view it all as it unfolds. Like a front-row seat at a shoot-'em-up movie, heaven affords spectators the perfect place from which to watch the death of earth. "We will be watching from the balconies of heaven," boasts Hagee.[5] Another believer writes, "Thank God, I will get a view of the Battle of Armageddon from the grandstand seats of the heavens. All who are born again will see the Battle of Armageddon, but it will be from the skies."[6]

Tim LaHaye and Jerry Jenkins' eleventh novel, *Armageddon*, introduces a new spectator angle for their pilot hero, Rayford Steele. He can now fly his plane over Armageddon and get the same bird's-eye aerial view of the battle site that raptured believers will see from heaven:

> That old curiosity was back. Rayford couldn't shake it. No way he could be this close to Armageddon—he guessed less than seventy miles—and not do a flyover. It was crazy, he knew. He might find himself in an air traffic jam. But the possibility of seeing an aerial view of what he had been hearing and reading and praying about drew him like an undertow. (LaHaye and Jenkins, *Armageddon*, 324)

This voyeuristic desire for an aerial view of the end of the world while escaping its torments is what dispensationalism is all about. Rayford's flyover epitomizes that desire.

The insights of former war correspondent Chris Hedges, in *War Is a Force That Gives Us Meaning*, can be helpful for shedding light on this voyeuristic desire for a violent ending to Revelation's story that believers can both escape and also watch. As war correspondent with the *Dallas Morning News* and the *New York Times*, Hedges covered wars in El Salvador, Bosnia, Kuwait, Iraq, and other countries. Hedges says that he became addicted to war. He craved the thrill and excitement. War was a drug for him—"the most powerful narcotic invented by humankind."

Hedges critiques our addiction to the television version of war today—a spectator sport. The "seductiveness of violence, the fascination with the grotesque—what the Bible calls 'the lust of the eye'—the god-like empowerment over other human lives" becomes almost mythic.[7] In mythic war "we fight absolutes. We must vanquish darkness." War becomes entertainment.

People love to watch violence. This "lust of the eye" is nothing new. In the early church, the theologian Tertullian counseled against Christian attendance at the violent spectacles and gladiatorial games of the Roman world. His extended treatise *De Spectaculis* points to the dangerous allure of watching violence. Christians need to train themselves not to watch, Tertullian says, not to be entranced by violence. Violence is mythic and seductive. It is a narcotic—like the "poison" or "sorcery" (the Greek word for "drug," *pharmakeia*) that Revelation says Rome administered to the world in order to deceive and intimidate people with its violence.[8] Violence draws us like an undertow, as Rayford found when he was unable to resist flying over Armageddon to watch the carnage.

"If you spend long enough in war," Hedges told Bill Moyers, "it's finally the only place you can feel at home. And that's, of course, a sickness. But I had it."[9]

Today's Christian fixation on Armageddon and war is also a sickness, even while it may be thrilling and entertaining. The dispensationalist storyline of blood and wrath must not become our home.

Only you can decide which version of the Lamb's story you want to follow—*Left Behind*'s version or the alternative. Amy Frykholm interviewed people who said, "I would only be persuaded by a different story." So I am seeking to tell that different story—the story of a God in whose heart is a Lamb.

Christian fundamentalists and *Left Behind* readers argue that the war story is the way Revelation's story must unfold. I argue that the Lamb's story gives us a very different model for God's storyline in our world today. Christian fundamentalists are willing to let the Middle East become the battleground. Simply put, we cannot afford to accept their version of the story. The violent ending they desire is not the Bible's vision for our world.

Rapture in Reverse

God's Vision for Renewing the World

SADLY, THE DISPENSATIONALIST timetable completely postpones any renewal or healing for the world until a distant time way off in the future. The return of Jesus as a warrior-like lion is the "main event" in their prophetic countdown.[1] The renewal of heaven and earth will just have to wait—more than a thousand years. And then, only after God has destroyed the earth. Dispensationalists clearly are not interested in any healing for the world.

The war story—the return to earth of an armed Christ, with his armies in chapter 19—this is what really interests them. They view the culmination of the book of Revelation as Christ's "Glorious Appearing" on a white horse to do battle and establish his millennial kingdom based in Jerusalem for one thousand years. The twelfth and final *Left Behind* novel culminates with this Glorious Appearing.

But chapter 19 is not the end of Revelation's story. We need to keep reading. By far the most important chapters in Revelation's vision for our world are chapters 21 and 22, the New Jerusalem vision. Beginning with the promises to the "victor" in the opening seven letters, the entire book pushes forward toward these chapters as the culminating vision of the book—the picture of our life together on earth in a renewed world. Revelation's New Jerusalem vision for our world is much like what the Rev. Dr. Martin Luther King Jr. called God's "beloved community."

Revelation wants to point us even now to the urgency of the New Jerusalem vision for this earth, a vision not reserved for one thousand years off in the future. The New Jerusalem vision is meant to be God's vision by which we live our lives right now, as followers of the Lamb and of Lamb power in our world. This power of God's New Jerusalem as a spiritual vision for communities today is something dispensationalists completely deny.

The apocalyptic journey in the middle chapters of Revelation takes readers through visions of judgment and plagues unleashed against the powers of evil and injustice in the world. Fortunately, those plagues and judgments are not the end of Revelation's story—nor is Armageddon. The key is to keep reading, keep listening all the way through to the end of the story, to the final vision of God's New Jerusalem.

The Lamb is leading us on an exodus out of the heart of empire, out of the heart of addiction to violence, greed, fear, an unjust lifestyle or whatever holds each of us most captive. It is an exodus we can experience each day. Tenderly, gently, the Lamb is guiding us to pastures of life and healing beside God's river. At the end of the book of Revelation, the New Jerusalem vision of Revelation 21–22 gives us a wonderful description of that new life with the Lamb.

The New Jerusalem vision takes us through two stages on the journey to the landscape of promise, both of which can be crucial for our life today. Our exodus journey is deeply spiritual, even mystical, with far-reaching political and ethical consequences. First of all we go in to worship, to the throne of God—into the heart of the

universe—to see the Lamb's vision of true power and life and salvation. Second, we return back home to the world, with our vision
transformed to see the world in a new way, transfigured in light of
the Lamb. This chapter will explore the first stage on that exodus
path, the journey inward.

THE MYSTICAL JOURNEY "IN"

Come with me now on another journey back to first-century Ephesus, this time to a house on a narrow back street. Christians were
such a tiny and marginal group in the first century that we don't
even know where they met for worship. There is no archeological
trace of the earliest churches until much later, in the fourth or fifth
centuries. Probably in the first centuries the Christians simply met
in homes.

One of our most intriguing sources of information about early
Christian meetings is furnished by a Roman governor in a province
north of Revelation's seven cities, who wrote a letter to the emper-
or asking him how to deal with this growing sect of Christianity.
Governor Pliny's letter dates to 120 A.D., one generation after Revelation and written almost a thousand miles away. Still, it might be
fairly accurate for Revelation's context as well. The letter certainly
shows the sense of political threat that Christianity posed to the
empire. Pliny wrote completely on hearsay about Christians, using
the best intelligence sources available to brief the emperor on this
new sect that was gaining converts:

> On a specified day before sunrise they were accustomed to gather
> and sing an antiphonal hymn to Christ as their god and to pledge
> themselves by an oath not to engage in any crime . . . They then
> went their separate ways, and came together later to eat a common
> meal. (*Letters of Pliny the Younger* 10.96; trans. Eugene Boring, *Reve-*

lation, Interpretation Commentaries [Louisville, Ken.: John Knox
Press, 1989], 14–15)

From Pliny's letter we glean information that can help us envision
life in the first century, confirming what we know from Revelation
itself both about the political risk of being a Christian and also the
central role of worship. Worship was held on the "Lord's Day" (Rev
1:10), but since Sunday was also a work day in the Roman Empire,
Christians gathered very early in the morning for worship. They dis-
persed and then came together again in the evening to share a "common meal," probably the Lord's Supper or eucharistic meal.

Who are these Christians? They were probably a multicultural
community, including many whose first language was not Greek.
Most were not citizens of the Roman Empire. The Cuban American scholar Justo Gonzales likens Revelation's multicultural perspective to *mestizo* literature, addressed to people of a "mixed" cultural heritage today.[2] They were an ethnically mixed group,
consisting of both Jewish Christians—perhaps including some
refugees displaced by the war in Palestine—and local Gentile Christians with long-time roots, some of whom were drawn first to
Judaism for its ethical teachings and its monotheism. This multicultural group comes together on a Sunday evening around their
heartfelt conviction that "Jesus has set up here on earth a community that is an alternative to empire," as Pablo Richard describes.[3]

People arrive for the evening service at the house in Ephesus
exhausted from work—whether toiling as slaves unloading ships in
the harbor, selling produce in the market, or as domestic or commercial workers. The community may also include a few merchants
or wealthier homeowners, although the overwhelming majority of
the populace was poor. They gather to pray and sing songs to God
and the Lamb, to share Bible stories and to break bread in remem-

brance of Jesus' death and resurrection. They come together around a radical and transforming vision of the joyful reign of God.

As the evening passes the worship service takes the Christians on a wonderful and life-changing journey, a journey that unfolds through the reading of a powerful letter from the prophetic leader John. John had visited their house church and was now on the island of Patmos. The whole experience of singing together, of hearing scripture, and then reading this prophetic letter mystically transports them on a visionary journey to the throne of God and the Lamb.

In the letter from John they hear a call to faithfulness, a call to renew their love for one another. They hear the promise that they will be victorious, provided that they resist the seductions of empire. They see a vision of living creatures singing praise to God around the throne. They hear the good news that "they will reign." They are transported to heaven not in the sense of escape or going away from earth, but in the sense of going more deeply *in*. Like Lucy and her companions going into New Narnia, in *The Last Battle,* the Christians of Ephesus go into the heart of the universe, into the heart of the world, into the heart of God. It is "world within world," as C. S. Lewis describes.[4] The mystical journey *in* pulls back the veil of everyday reality in Ephesus so that they can see true reality, so that they can go more deeply into God's picture.

At the center of the throne they see Jesus, the Lamb, leading them to springs of water, accompanying them in every struggle. They see a vision of God's beloved city, a city that comes down for them as a gift—a city of healing and hope more real than reality itself. Despite the system of injustice and powerlessness in which they live, Revelation invites these beleaguered Christians to enter into God's beloved city as full citizens and royal heirs. After all their long days of backbreaking labor, after hearing judgment and intimidation all around them, this culminating vision of Revelation now gathers them together beside God's riverside, to drink of its water of life, to find shelter beside God's majestic tree of life with its healing leaves. Revelation invites them to dream about their world in light of God's story and God's vision for the future.

It is the power of John's words to take people on this transformative journey, to lead them to the throne of God and the Lamb in the beloved city. Like a virtual tour of a place never visited, but longed for, the first-century Christians are invited to close their eyes—or rather open their eyes!—and go with John on this tour of God's beloved city in Revelation 21–22.

> Then one of the seven angels . . . said to me, "Come I will show you the bride, the wife of the Lamb." And in the spirit he carried me away to a great high mountain and showed me the holy city Jerusalem coming down out of heaven from God. It has the glory of God and a radiance like a very rare jewel. (Rev 21:9–11)

Belief in such a heavenly Jerusalem, often personified as a bride or mother, was widespread in biblical times. Jewish Christians in John's churches would have been familiar with promises of such a heavenly city from the prophet Isaiah and from other apocalypses. Even the apostle Paul took this belief for granted in Galatians: "Jerusalem above . . . is our mother" (Gal 4:26). Especially after the destruction of Jerusalem by the Romans in 70 A.D., dreams of a heavenly city flourished among Jews and Christians.

What is striking in Revelation, in contrast to every other ancient text, is that this heavenly city of Jerusalem does not stay up in heaven but rather *comes down* from heaven to earth.

The city that descends from heaven is a welcoming and beautiful city, its radiance like a rare jewel. Picture Dorothy and her companions finally reaching the Emerald City in the movie *The Wizard of Oz*, after all their peril and tribulations along the way. Such was the joy early Christians must also have experienced in hearing the story of John's New Jerusalem vision for the first time. It assured them of another world, the reign of God, an alternative citizenship to Rome's that was far more true and just.

This is how God's wondrous city beckons to us as we approach on our tour. Our whole life we have been following the river that leads us here, to life in God's holy city of beauty and healing. We see the city from afar, with its foundations and gates gleaming with emerald and other precious stones. We see the river, we see the beautiful open gates. We want to go in! We long to see God and the Lamb face to face!

As you read Revelation 21–22, imagine yourself walking into this city through its open gates, exploring the landscape that the angel unfolds before you. You are safe at last. You are beloved. You need not fear death any longer, nor economic insecurity nor oppression nor any terror. Savor the experience of walking through the pearly gates, onto the city's majestic golden streets, as your angelic guide leads you around. Drink in the vision. Let yourself fall in love with this city as you let go of all ties to the violence and injustice of empire today. This vision is the culmination of Revelation's whole life-changing journey. In this city, all of God's promises come to fulfillment for you.

RAPTURE IN REVERSE: GOD'S DWELLING WITH US ON EARTH

Contrary to the dispensationalist view, there is no rapture in the story of Revelation, no snatching of people off the earth up to heaven. Look at it this way: it is God who is Raptured down to earth to take up residence and dwell with us—a Rapture in reverse:

> And I saw the holy city, the new Jerusalem, coming down out of
> heaven from God, prepared as a bride . . . And I heard a loud voice
> from the throne saying "See, the dwelling of God is among mortals.
> God will dwell with them as their God; they will be his people, and
> God's very self will be with them." (Rev 21:2–3)

"Heaven" is not mentioned again in the book of Revelation after
Revelation 21:2—a fact especially striking for a book in which heav-
en has been so central. This is because God's throne moves down to
earth. The New Jerusalem of Revelation 21–22 is a wonderfully
earth-centered vision of our future, a vision of hope for this world.
Contrary to the escapism and "heavenism" that dominates fundamentalist interpretations today, the storyline of Revelation emphasizes that our future dwelling will be with God on earth, in a radiant, thriving city landscape.[5] The home of God is among people.
From now on, God "will dwell with them as their God."

The word "dwell" in Revelation is the same word as used to
describe Jesus' coming to earth in the Gospel of John, "the Word
became flesh and dwelt among us." The whole message of the
Bible is that God loves the world so much that God comes to earth
to dwell with us. The Gospel of Matthew calls Jesus "Emmanuel,"
which means in Hebrew "God is with us." Revelation proclaims
that same message of God's dwelling in our world. It is the message that God's home is no longer up in heaven, but here in our
midst, incarnate on earth. In Revelation 21–22 God's throne moves
down out of heaven, where it was in chapter 4, and is now located
in the midst of the city—in the city descended down *out of* heaven,
down to earth.

The message of God's dwelling in the world is not a message
reserved for thousands of years off in the future. The dispensationalist script insists that a lengthy predetermined sequence of cat-

aclysmic events must happen before God's New Jerusalem vision can dawn in our world: first the Rapture; then the seven years of tribulation, then the thousand-year millennial reign, then the last judgment, and only then will God's New Jerusalem come to earth for the privileged few who survive. Dispensationalists put New Jerusalem way off into the distant future.

But biblical prophecy and apocalypses do not operate according to such a rigid sequential timetable. Revelation gives us a vision, not a chronology of predictions. God and the Lamb *already* reign, Revelation insists from the very outset. "The kingdom of the world *has become* the kingdom of our Lord and of his Messiah," the angel proclaimed after the seventh trumpet (Rev 11:15). Jesus is already the "king over the kings of the earth," as chapter 1 introduces him. While Christ's reign is not yet fully realized, God gives us glimpses of it even now, even while we wait for it to fully unfold in the future.

God's people always live in a tension between the "already" and "not yet" of God's reign—a tension that Revelation keeps alive. Revelation's New Jerusalem offers both a future hope and a present reality that is breaking into our world even now. God's time is not linear—as we see when God speaks from the throne to enfold past and present and future into one wonderful, sweeping declaration: "I am the Alpha and the Omega, the beginning and the end" (Rev 21:6). Revelation invites us to enter into God's vision for our world even now, and to live in terms of this vision. Such a journey into God's vision happens in communion with God, in mystical experiences of Scripture coming to life, when you let go of the flat page and go deeply into the picture. It is not a linear kind of seeing that takes you to God's city. It is a mystical, liberating kind of sight—like the deeper dimension of a three-dimensional Magic Eye picture—that Revelation desires for each one of us.

In one of his last sermons before he was assassinated, the Rev. Dr. Martin Luther King conveyed this sense of New Jerusalem as both a future and present reality, a wondrous vision for justice in which we can participate even now: "Thank God for John, who centuries ago out on a lonely, obscure island called Patmos caught vision of a new Jerusalem descending out of heaven from God, who heard a voice saying, 'Behold I make all things new—former things are passed away. God grant that we will be participants in this newness . . . If we will but do it, we will bring about a new day of justice and brotherhood and peace. And that day the morning stars will sing together.'"[6]

TOUR OF THE CITY

Led by an angelic guide, we become participants in New Jerusalem's newness. The book's final vision takes us on a tour of God's beloved city—a life-changing journey to the heart of God. Like a travel guide-book, Revelation 21–22 shows us each detail of the city to help us appreciate more fully the landscape of God and our own place in it. Look around the city. What features do you notice on the tour? The angel wants to show us a city of beauty and wholeness. Notice that everywhere in this amazing city we are in the presence of a loving God here on earth. There is no temple, a very unusual feature for an ancient city. Instead, the entire city is a place of holiness. God and the Lamb are themselves the light for the city, and also its temple.

> I saw no temple in the city, for its temple is the Lord God the Almighty and the Lamb. And the city has no need of sun or moon to shine on it, for the glory of God is its light, and its lamp is the Lamb. (Rev 21:22–23)

Like the grandest cities of the ancient world, this city has a wall—but it is not a wall to keep anyone out, since its twelve gates are always open.

Its gates will never be shut by day—and there will be no night there. People will bring into it the glory and the honor of the nations. (Rev 21:25–26)

New Jerusalem is a welcoming city, not a gated community—an important message for our time when nations build walls to keep out immigrants and foreigners. The walls give the city beauty and radiance, with twelve gates of translucent pearl that always stand open. This city is home for the whole world, open to all nations and peoples. The twelve gates in the wall symbolize the foundation of the city on the Bible's twelve tribes and twelve apostles. Indeed, the whole vision of the city is founded on Israel and its scriptures, opened up now to welcome in all nations.

Some things are left outside the city's walls. Everything about the old order of fear and domination, of imperial violence and injustice, must be left behind. A whole series of contrasts listed with the phrase "no more" underscores the newness of the political economy of God's city compared with the exploitive economy of Babylon/Rome: "Death will be no more; mourning and crying and pain will be no more, for the first things have passed away." And God will wipe away every tear. Threats in Revelation 21:8 and 21:27 convey a sense of urgency, a prophetic wake-up call. As I have argued, the function of such threats is exhortation to faithfulness, not prediction. Revelation poses an urgent life-or-death choice between the beast's way of the life and that of the Lamb. We must leave behind everything that is violent or unjust, so that we can be among those who enter as citizens into God's holy city, so that our names are written in the Lamb's book of life.

RIVER OF LIFE

Continue the journey still more deeply into God's picture, led by the angelic tour guide. In the center of the city a paradise of green space and water opens up. A river of life flows through the city's midst, giving life to everything it touches. Think of your favorite river, the clearest and most beautiful stream that you have ever seen—that is a vision of Revelation's river of life, freely given for all who are thirsty and weary. You are invited to come to this wonderful riverside.

In one of my favorite visions of scripture the prophet Ezekiel describes an ever-deepening river flowing from the temple. It is tree-lined river, full of life and fish, bringing life to everything the river touches.[7] Revelation builds on Ezekiel's nourishing river, describing an even more expansive vision:

> Then the angel showed me the river of the water of life, bright as crystal, flowing from the throne of God and of the Lamb through the middle of the street of the city. On either side of the river is the tree of life with its twelve kinds of fruit, producing its fruit each month; and the leaves of the tree are for the healing of the nations. (Rev 22:1–2)

Water abounds in the landscape of New Jerusalem, flowing "without price" for everyone who thirsts. Twice God extends the invitation to come and take the water of life without money or payment—"as a gift" — the Greek word *dorean*: "To the one who is thirsty I will give to drink from the spring of the water of life as a gift." This promise is reiterated in chapter 22: "Let everyone who is thirsty come. Let anyone who desires take the water of life as a gift" (Rev 22:17; Rev 21:6). These wonderful invitations echo the prophet Isaiah who invited everyone who thirsts to "come to the waters . . . and you that have no money, come, buy and eat" (Isa 55:1).

Why so much talk of "without money"? Because Revelation knows that poor people lack the money to buy even the essentials of life. Revelation's vision is for everyone. This is the water of life for which we are longing, for which we are "thirsty, soul-thirsty." It is spiritual water, but more than spiritual—it also has something to say to the real rivers and waters that give life to our world.[8] For people to whom even the cost of water is unaffordable, the fact that God gives the water of life without payment comes as good news. As a healing contrast to the exploitive economy of Babylon, New Jerusalem offers a gift economy in which water and other essentials of life are given "without cost."

In other ways as well, the landscape of God's city contrasts sharply with that of the evil city of Babylon/Rome, a political economy that was characterized by violence and ecological injustice. In the unfolding imagery of Revelation, the invitation to drink from the "spring" of the water of life functions as a contrast to the deadly "springs" of waters that turned to blood and became undrinkable in the plague sequence (Rev 16:4). Paradise-like images of nature and healing describe a sort of re-creation of the garden of Eden in the center of this huge urban landscape. New Jerusalem invites us, like an oasis after all the terror of Babylon/Rome. Here in this city God and nature and human beings are all reconciled, the culmination of Revelation's story.[9]

Revelation's river of life recalls the rivers of Eden and all the other rivers that flow through the Bible. It is the spiritual confluence of the prophet Ezekiel's ever-deepening river from the temple, the prophet Zechariah's flowing fountain, the river of Psalm 46—"There is a river whose streams make glad the city of God"— and even Jesus' promise to everyone who thirsts that "rivers of living water" will flow out of their heart.[10]

Notice the source from which Revelation's life-giving river flows. Since Revelation has stated that there is "no temple" in the holy city, the river of life flows out not from the temple as in Ezekiel but from "throne of God and of the Lamb."

HEALING OUR WOUNDS: THE TREE OF LIFE

What else do you see at God's riverside? Notice the wonderful tree of life flourishing on both banks of the river of life. This tree is one of the most powerful images of the book of Revelation—the subject of both the promise to "the victor" in the church in Ephesus and also the final warning in the book's closing verses. The tree of life frames the entire book. Revelation wants you to share in God's tree of life—to rest in its shade, to eat of its fruit, and to be healed of every wound by its medicinal leaves.

Look up into the tree's branches and see the succulent fruit growing all year long. Can we eat this fruit? Can we touch? These are important questions, because in the Genesis story of creation God specifically told Adam and Eve that the fruit from this tree of life was forbidden. Revelation lifts the Genesis prohibition. The promise to the church in Ephesus is that God's people can now eat of the fruit of the tree of life, a promise of life even better than the Garden of Eden: "To the one who conquers I will give to eat of the fruit of the tree of life that is in the paradise of my God" (Rev 2:7).

Think how wonderful this promise of unlimited food must have been in the face of the poverty and hunger that haunted many of John's communities in the first century: abundant fruit, an ever-bearing tree, growing beside the river of life with its water flowing as a gift for everyone. In contrast to the economy of Babylon/ Rome, which was characterized by famine and hunger and an exploitive system of taxation that squeezed peasants and the poor, God's holy city provides enough food to all. How does this speak to your deepest hunger, as well as to the hunger of our world?

Look more closely at the leaves on the tree of life. Revelation tells us that these leaves are medicine—the Greek word *therapeia*, like therapy or healing—in contrast to the toxic drugs (the Greek word *pharmakeia*) that evil Babylon/Rome used to poison the world. "The leaves of the tree are for the healing of the nations," Revelation says. These healing leaves may be based on ancient knowledge of certain trees' actual medicinal properties. Many cultures have healing trees still today.[11] Whether based on a literal or a more metaphorical imagery of spiritual healing, the tree of life brings healing for our world and for each one of us. That is the very heart of the Revelation's message for us today—that God wants to heal our world.

What are your wounds? What is it in your life that most needs healing? Are you carrying a terrible burden of pain? Are you grieving the death of a loved one? Are you haunted by suffering in the world? The grief I carry most deeply is our destruction of the world's environment, the death of forests and species and the impending end to so many beautiful places through the results of global warming. It is an urgent, even aching concern for me, and I long to see healing for the planet and for all its wounded places.

Revelation invites us to lay the healing leaves of the tree onto every physical and spiritual wound we carry. The tree of life is a wonderful image of healing. I think back to the nurse in Bethlehem whose work is wound care. Picture God caring for you like that, tenderly placing leaves on you and on the world with healing power to knit back together even your deepest brokenness. Picture the tree's leaves bringing healing to wounded relationships, to wounded families, to communities and nations—healing global warming and our culture's insatiable greed. God wants to bring the healing power of these medicinal leaves to our entire broken world. Poet George McDonald wrote about his struggle to pray, and used the image of a bird coming to lay God's healing leaves on his heart:

> Sometimes, hard trying it seems I cannot pray . . . Yet some half-fledged prayer-bird from the nest may fall, flit, fly, perch—crouch in the bowery breast of the large, nation-healing tree of life. Moveless there sit through the burning day and on my heart at night a fresh leaf cooling lay. (George McDonald, *Diary of An Old Soul*; quoted in *Diary of An Old Soul: 366 Writings for Devotional Reflection* [Minneapolis, Minn.: Fortress Press, 1994], entry for January 14)

Notice that healing in Revelation comes not directly from God or the Lamb, not from some absent future time, but through the actual created world—through the leaves of a living tree. This is another signal of how God loves creation and still calls it good—an important corrective to the vast dispensationalist imagery of destruction.

Healing is not just for individuals, on this Revelation is very clear. God's healing is for the whole world, for all peoples as well as for the earth. Revelation models its tree and its healing on Ezekiel chapter 47, but Revelation deliberately expands the prophet Ezekiel's vision to draw in all nations, not just Israel. Ezekiel's healing leaves have become "leaves for the healing of the *nations*" in Revelation. Look around our world today and picture all the places in need of healing. Picture all the nations walking by the Lamb's light, into the beloved city. Contrary to the gospel of dispensation-alism and *Left Behind*, God plans to heal the nations of the world, not destroy them.

SHARING IN GOD'S HEALING REIGN

The tour of the city concludes with a vision of every one of us—God's beloved servants—worshiping before the throne of the Lamb and sharing in God's reign:

> Nothing accursed will be found there any more. But the throne of God and of the Lamb will be in it, and his servants will worship him; they will see his face, and his name will be on their foreheads. And there will be no more night; they need no light of lamp or sun, for the Lord God will be their light, and they will reign forever and ever. (Rev 22:3–5)

God's servants or slaves shall reign forever and ever, Revelation declares. We are royalty—kings and queens, like that old margarine commercial where a crown appears on your head when you spread it on your breakfast toast.

At a time when Rome claimed to reign victoriously over the entire world, Revelation boldly proclaimed that God and the Lamb are the ones who reign—not the Roman Empire, not any other empire—and that God's servants also reign with them. Recall that Ephesus was a center of slave trade, and early Christians lived in a society in which as many as 30 percent of the empire's people were slaves—ruled over by someone who had total control over their lives. Here John assures them that even slaves will rule as royalty in God's reign. Think how empowering this promise of reigning must have been for powerless people at the time it was written. In the same way, it empowers the most marginalized and powerless people in our world today.

Yet God's servants do not reign *over* anyone else. It is not a sense of dominion over any other people or over creation. This verse invites us to explore ways we can understand our reign not as domination but as sharing in God's healing for the world. We reign as servants of God's own healing power.

In New Jerusalem, God gives us a vision for our world, a vision we can claim as heirs: "Those who conquer will inherit these things, and I will be their God and they will be my children" (Rev 21:7). Everything the angel showed us on our tour—every corner of this beautiful city with its wondrous river and healing tree of life—becomes our inheritance.

Through nonviolent Lamb power and through our testimony, we have "conquered." The beast is defeated and Babylon/Rome has been tried and sentenced in the divine courtroom. God now invites us to enter into the holy city as heirs and as beloved children. The good news is that we can already taste and see God's vision. The Spirit and the bridal city are already inviting us to "Come!" All we have to do is follow the Lamb to the riverside. Come into God's new world!

The Journey Outward

Homecoming to the World

O UR TOUR OF THE CITY IS COMPLETE. The angel has
shown us every corner of the beloved city, with a beauty and
radiance surpassing our dreams. This mystical journey to the holy
city and the throne of God in Revelation 21–22 fulfills the first
stage of our exodus in Revelation.

In a strange and wonderful way, God shows the ancient Christians, and us today, that the throne of the Lamb is already in the
midst of us, in our own community, and that renewal of the world
will come from the river that flows forth from that throne. Everything is changed as we view the earth anew in light of our saving
God.

Dispensationalist writers consign Revelation's New Jerusalem
vision to some far-off future. In the interim, these authors typical-
ly create an idyllic paradise for the born-again Jewish remnant in
the red-rock city of Petra—located in what they say is the biblical
land of "Edom"—in Jordan, not far from Israel. The Antichrist's

bombs and missiles cannot harm *Left Behind*'s born-again Christian Jews in the rustic, high-tech haven of Petra. Rayford's helicopters can miraculously take off and land in the midst of a shower of bullets, while all-terrain vehicles for navigating the cliff city's rock staircases and narrow streets are plentiful. Some readers identify with this sense of refuge and safety, a special place where manna falls from heaven and biblical miracles still occur. In *Left Behind*'s story, born-again Christians set up a huge tech center in Petra with round-the-clock Internet evangelism from the cliff dwellings, while outside people discuss Bible verses around the campfire.

But none of this Petra geography has any basis in Revelation or in the Bible. I love to visit Petra—it is a fabulous ancient city—but we do not have to go to any "special place" to find the safety and life envisioned in God's New Jerusalem. Rather, the New Jerusalem vision of Revelation 21–22 gives a vision for every community, for every place. Revelation's vision for our own place—our journey homeward—will be the second part of our exodus journey.

THE MYSTICAL JOURNEY OF WORSHIP

The mystical journey into the "Aha" presence of God's New Jerusalem and its river of life can happen in many ways for you: through nature, when you behold a mountain or stream so beautiful that it transports you to God's riverside; through music that connects you mystically to heavenly chorus; or through other powerful experiences of community or presence that take you outside of yourself. A wonderful, sacramental sense of holiness pervades the entire New Jerusalem vision and our world as well. Writer Annie Dillard describes such experiences of God's shimmering holiness as "seeing the tree with lights on it," drawing on the words of a woman after cataract surgery who was able to see the world for the first time.[1] Our world is full of those experiences of the sacred, Dillard reminds us—these "Aha" glimpses of revelation that transport us more deeply into God's picture.

Revelation gives us eyes to see God's tree with lights on it, the biblical tree of life in our midst! Revelation gives us eyes to see the whole world with a kind of sacramental vision.

One of the most powerful ways to experience such a sacramental vision is through worship. Whether in first-century Ephesus or in the place where you live today, the "Aha" experience of worship takes you on an apocalyptic journey again and again, bringing Revelation's visions to life through singing, praying, hearing the words of scripture, and sharing in bread and wine. In the liturgy you actually go into heaven to taste and see God's water of life, given without price. You gather with God's people at the river, you join with all the living creatures in praising God around the throne. You journey with them to the radiant, holy city, and you taste its gifts, given for you.

A Greek Orthodox friend once explained his understanding of the liturgy of holy communion, how a whole cloud of angels and living creatures and all of heaven surrounds the altar, mystically singing the "Holy, holy, holy" along with the congregation on earth and the communion of saints and witnesses through the ages. The future merges with the present in just such a way in Revelation's songs and prayers. In communion with God and with one another, God's holy city takes form as a concrete vision of hope for our world.

As Revelation's journey draws toward its conclusion, the Spirit and the bridal New Jerusalem invite everyone who thirsts to come:

> The Spirit and the bride say, "Come." And let everyone who hears say, "Come." And let everyone who is thirsty come. Let anyone who wishes take the water of life as a gift. (Rev 22:17)

Some scholars identify this verse from Revelation 22:17 as a fragment of very early liturgical dialogue from a Christian worship service in John's churches.[2] This was probably the invitation to the holy communion feast or Lord's Supper, a foretaste of the Lamb's marriage banquet and the gifts of the beloved city. Similar to the call-and-response style of an African-American preacher interacting with the congregation, this dialogue links us even now to God's city and to God's river of life as they call out to us to "come."

We do not know the details of how the earliest Christians celebrated their communion liturgy, but Pliny's letter makes it clear that they shared a meal. References to "manna" in Revelation's opening letters also point to that experience of worship. Perhaps water was part of that communion meal, in addition to bread and wine. Revelation's closing chapters invite us to desire God's pure water of life, intensely and personally given in a living encounter.

The invitation to drink of God's water makes the crucial connection outward, to the second stage of our life-changing apocalyptic journey—the return to earth. We long to stay around the throne, in the presence of the Lamb, in the beloved paradise of God. But the journey is ending. We are being transported back to home, back to earth, just as the first-century Christians realized that they were not in heaven after all—they were only in Ephesus, back where they had been all along. Like Dorothy in *The Wizard of Oz*, they wake up to find that they are still in the equivalent of Kansas, and that they never left home. It was all a vision . . . but what a vision! A life-changing vision, every bit as transformative as Scrooge's fateful nightmare. Gathered at the riverside, God's people have tasted life-giving water and manna from heaven. They have glimpsed God's beloved city. Because of that, everything is different now. Everything is precious.

As the Christians in Ephesus listened to Revelation read aloud in the worship service they traveled with John on a life-changing apocalyptic journey. The journey opened their eyes to see the world and their home differently. The journey also gave them a blessing: "Blessed is the one who reads aloud the words of this prophecy, and blessed are those who hear and keep what is written in it." Now the challenge is to live their whole life according to the story of God's beloved city, to "keep what is written" and live in terms of its blessing.

As they come back from behind the apocalyptic veil, the Christians of Ephesus now see their own city more dearly, glimpsed in a new and deeper way. Like Scrooge waking up from his visions or Dorothy waking up in Kansas, everything is different now because of their life-changing apocalyptic journey. The street on which they live is still just as narrow and crowded as before, but they now see their narrow street transfigured in light of the street in God's holy city. They now see the Lamb standing in the middle of the street, looking at them with eyes of love. In the scrawny little tree at the end of their street they catch a glimpse of God's tree of life with its healing leaves. In the cry of the neighbor's hungry baby they hear the cry of God on behalf of our world. Most important, they now see that God's home or dwelling is in their midst.

It is difficult to believe at times, this vision of Revelation. But the apocalyptic journey has persuaded the Christians of Ephesus that the throne of God is in the middle of their city and that a wondrous river flows out from that throne to renew the whole earth. Their entire geography is changed now, in light of what they have seen—in light of the landscape of God's salvation, God's holy city, paradise itself, in their midst.

That is how we, too, are meant to glimpse and live in terms of the landscape of New Jerusalem today. Now that we have experienced the biblical river of life we can see that it flows right through our city—through Chicago and Kansas, or wherever we live. Our own geography is different now that we have seen the vision of God's dwelling in our midst, on earth. Now we see not just our daily commute between home and office, our noisy corner where the homeless man huddles for warmth, our suburban mall or even the well-manicured country club, but we see a Lamb standing in the midst of the neighborhood, we see Jesus in our community.

God's beloved city in Revelation 21–22 is not primarily a vision for after we die, or for after Jesus returns. It is rather a vision that can transform the way we live out God's reign in the world today. It is a vision of the healing leaves that God wants to lay on every broken heart, on every war-torn landscape. It is a vision of Lamb power in the world. And we are part of that vision. Once we have seen the new creation, the joy of that experience must inform everything that we do.[3]

IMAGINING NEW JERUSALEM

The vision of God's New Jerusalem—of a holy city with gleaming, golden streets and pearly gates, where death and tears are no more—has given form and voice to the dreams of God's people through the ages. From Saint Augustine's "City of God" to African-American spirituals and gospel songs, Revelation's holy city has inspired people's hopes for healing and renewal. The eighteenth-century poet William Blake was fascinated and inspired by Revelation. He used the image of New Jerusalem to criticize the hideous factories and inhuman working conditions of England's industrial revolution: "Was Jerusalem builded here Among these dark Satanic Mills? . . . I will not cease from Mental Fight . . . Till we have built Jerusalem in England's green & pleasant Land."[4] The vision fed early American visions of a "city on a hill" and a range of nineteenth-century utopian experiments. Throughout history, people have sought to live in terms of God's holy city and its idyllic peace.

Longing for New Jerusalem is the subject of some of the most powerful African-American spirituals. "Gonna put on those golden shoes down by the riverside," sings one favorite song. Where is that riverside? Is it in a world we experience only after we die? Is it a far-off time that we can only sing about? For slaves, the New Jerusalem vision gave hope for freedom even in this life, for a riverside not just in heaven but experienced also as a very real river in their lives that could be crossed to freedom, here and now. They found a glimpse of the riverside of God in the geography of their place. That crossing between the two worlds is key to God's New Jerusalem for us as well.

Sometimes the contrast between the geography of our place and the geography of New Jerusalem underscores the reality of injustice. The Rev. Dr. Martin Luther King Jr. contrasted the hunger and poverty he saw in Memphis, Tennessee, in the 1960s to the New Jerusalem vision of Revelation 21:

> It's alright to talk about "streets flowing with milk and honey," but God has commanded us to be concerned about the slums down here, and his children who can't eat three square meals a day. It's all right to talk about the new Jerusalem, but one day, God's preacher must talk about the New York, the new Atlanta, the new Philadelphia, the new Los Angeles, the new Memphis, Tennessee. This is what we have to do. (Martin Luther King Jr., "I See the Promised Land," April 3, 1968, Memphis, Tennessee [Washington, *A Testament of Hope*, 282])

With its rich store of images, the book of Revelation can help us dream and work concretely for our own New Chicago, New Oakland, and New Tulsa in light of God's vision. Revelation gives us God's urgent message of hope for all the world's cities and communities. It promises a vision for our life in God after we die. But even more importantly, New Jerusalem holds promise for *this* world, giving a vision for "what we have to do," in the words of King.

I like to ask people to say the name of their own town or city out loud. Then I invite them to re-phrase the vision of New Jerusalem in terms of their own city's renewal, like King's vision of the New Philadelphia, the New Los Angeles: "I saw the holy city, God's New *(Name of Your Town)* coming down out of heaven . . ." What would your "new" city look like, envisioned in light of God's vision of hope? This is an exercise in "borrowing the eyes of God," as the German theologian Dorothee Soelle describes our mystical sight. We see our world as God sees it.[5] This is what happens in Revelation's New Jerusalem vision.

A student at the seminary where I teach led such an exercise with the people of Our Saviour's Lutheran Church in a blighted neighborhood of East Boston. Her question, "What might the new East Boston look like?" is an example of the kind of imagining of the New Jerusalem vision that can empower urban ministry today. She writes:

> "What does our city look like?" I asked this question of our Bible study group one Wednesday evening . . . I hardly had to wait for a response: stinky; scary; there are gangs . . . people are crying because they are hungry . . . there is poverty; people are homeless; it's unsafe . . . It seems a far cry from the glorious, radiant new Jerusalem.

"Where is that holy city where God dwells among the people?" I asked. They replied: The promised city must be describing heaven. It's something we look forward to, in the future, after we die. It's impossible now, they said.

Then I asked the group, "Can we try to imagine what the holy city, what the new East Boston might look like?" The people were quiet . . . and in the end this is what they said: "We saw the holy city, the new East Boston, coming down out of heaven from God . . . It has clean streets in which people can walk in safety and with peace at any time. There are no drugs, no fire, no fighting; no one is hungry; everyone has a place to live. People are planting flowers and trees . . . and God is there."

"These dreams ands hopes, are important," concludes Beth Utto-Galarneau as she describes helping children in a public housing project draw pictures of their dreams. "We have to keep hoping, imagining a better neighborhood, a holy city." (Beth Utto Gelarneau, *New England Synod Lutheran* [Worcester, Mass.: Winter, 1992])

We have to keep imagining the New Jerusalem in our world, and help others envision it, too. We have to see that the Lamb is beside us at every moment, standing on our corner, transforming the way we live. This is how we experience "Scripture coming to life," fulfilling the hunger for God's presence that *Left Behind* readers express. This is how we make connections between the Bible's storyline and our world—not in the violent Red Horse of the Apocalypse but in Revelation's vision for life in communion with God and one another in the holy city. Now that we see the Lamb in our midst everything is different. Listen for what Revelation's New Jerusalem vision has to say for your city, for riverside. Our calling as Christians is to live our life in terms of such connections.

RIVERS OF OUR LIVES

The rivers of our lives are some of the best places to see connections to God's vision for our world. A pillar on a bridge over the Charles River in Boston bears an inscription from Revelation 22 about the river of life in the holy city: "On either side of the river there was the tree of life which bears twelve manner of fruits . . . and the leaves of the tree of life were for the healing of the nations." When I first saw that inscription it seemed grandiose, even idolatrous. How could Bostonians claim such an explicit link between their river and God's river? But I have come to see the importance of such links for helping us see biblical connections to our world, to see our geography with new eyes. When we can glimpse in every river the river of life flowing from God's throne in the holy city, then we see ourselves as citizens, as stewards of earth's rivers and trees. Boston is not God's New Jerusalem, to be sure, but there is nonetheless a link between Boston's Charles River and God's river in the Bible's mystical geography of life.

By whatever name—the Charles River, the Mississippi, the Colorado, the Columbia—the biblical river of God flows from the throne through the middle of every city of the world. All our rivers are all connected to God's watershed of the river of life.

Bishop William Skylstad of the Roman Catholic Diocese of Spokane, Washington saw a glimpse of God's river of life flowing in the mighty Columbia River that flows through the Pacific Northwest. Grounded in a sacramental vision of the river's beauty and holiness, Bishop Skylstad guided a difficult pastoral-letterwriting process that brought together farmers, orchardists, hydro-electric utility leaders, environmentalists, Native Americans, and other residents to forge a common vision of the Columbia watershed as a "sacramental commons."[6] The document's ecological ethic seeks to give voice to endangered salmon and every other creature that makes its home in the Columbia watershed. "Our river of life-giving water is the mighty Columbia, an extraordinary treasure," writes Skylstad.[7] Bishop Skylstad traces his own vision for the Columbia River to growing up in northern Washington along the beautiful Methow River, a tributary of the Columbia.

At times, God's river of life may seem completely dried up. Someone in Chicago told me that there used to be a creek flowing through our neighborhood, but it has now been put into a pipe and paved over. "Follow the cottonwoods," the man told me, "and that's how you can see where the stream once was." Even when God's river has gone underground in our lives, it can still be found. Our task is to look for traces of that river—traces such as those cottonwoods—to see how Scripture is coming to life in a river of life flowing under our feet.

Revelation's vision for us, for our world, is a vision in which we do not leave earth behind. Instead, we go more deeply into the world—into the world that God created and still calls "good." We follow the river flowing under our feet; we see the world with new eyes. The message of Revelation is that the place where we will see the river of God flowing from the throne is *in* the world, in the middle of our city. The storyline of Revelation ends on earth.

New Jerusalem gives us a vision of a beloved community, a world of abundance for all. This is God's vision for our whole created world—a world where people of all nations find open gates of welcome, where poor people find water without price, where all find healing . . . a world that will not be left behind. This is a vision to which we are transported in worship. And this story also transports us back home to see and live God's vision in our world today.

God does not envision a solitary beauty for us as followers of the Lamb. Our mystical journey into God's New Jerusalem must transform the way we live together, in community, in the world. Revelation stresses this fact by locating the river of God in the *city*—the Greek word *polis* or "city" is the word from which we get our word "political." "God wills to restore this world to a beauty we can scarcely imagine," emphasizes Kathleen Norris. "It is a city, not a solitude, an important distinction in the narcissistic din of American culture."[8]

In every time and place, Revelation calls on us to "come out" of the beast's realm of violence and injustice so that we can participate in the beloved city of God. That call to "come out" in Revelation 18:4 is the key to Revelation's ethical imperative. The book wants us to follow the Lamb in a life-changing exodus. In the New Jerusalem vision Revelation teaches us how we can enter already into God's vision for our lives, through a sacramental way of life that pervades each moment. Revelation teaches us the lifestyle of nonviolent Lamb power—life according to a different geography, a different citizenship in an amazing city of beauty and healing for our world.

APOCALYPTIC HOPE

Revelation is not a book written to inspire fear or terror. But it is definitely written to increase a sense of urgency for our world. It is an apocalyptic wake-up call for each of us, precisely because there *is* hope for us and for our world.

Hope is surely Revelation's most profound contribution to our world today. Revelation teaches us a fierce, urgent, and wonderful hope—not an easy comfort, but a hope that knows the reality of terror and evil and still can testify to God's love in the face of that terror.

The hope of Revelation centers around the slain-yet-standing Lamb who has conquered—and around everything that that Lamb represents in God's vision for us and for the world. The Lamb who replaces the expected lion in Revelation's storyline continues to dwell with us and to overturn all the structures of war and injustice. In the face of empire, Revelation teaches us a way of life that is "Lamb power"—the power of nonviolent love to change the world. The hope of Revelation is simply this: that the Lamb has conquered the beast and that a wondrous river of life now flows out from the Lamb's throne to bring healing water to every corner of our wounded world.

Think of the book of Revelation as a life-transforming journey, a journey that we can go on each day. The book is prophetic in the sense that it speaks God's word of "timely warning" to our world and lays out contrasting visions for the future. It is apocalyptic in the sense that it actually takes us on journeys into each of these contrasting visions, to see and experience God's threats of judgment as well as God's vision of salvation. On the one hand Revelation's apocalyptic tours show us cosmic wake-up calls for our world more vivid than the terrors that Scrooge experienced. On the other hand, the book's vision of the beloved city of God unveils the Lamb's way of life in breathtaking beauty and almost irresistible wonder. It is the book's final vision—God's New Jerusalem—that the book promises for our world, and invites us to follow each day.

What is the message of Revelation for our world? That is the question on which the violent dispensationalist storyline must be challenged. Revelation is not about an inevitable doomsday for the earth nor about the Rapture. Revelation's story is about seeing the Lamb beside you in every moment of your life—in the car, at the shopping mall, at work or school. Revelation is about looking more deeply into God's picture and seeing how the Lamb is leading you even now into a world of joy and healing. That is how scripture comes to life for you—not in the Red Horse of the Apocalypse but in the Lamb's river of life, in the tree of life beside the river, with its leaves for the healing of the whole world.

As Martin Luther declares, living in the end-times means planting that tree even on the last day.

DEBUNKING THE RAPTURE BY VERSE

"We are not playing a game of biblical hopscotch," claims Hal Lindsey.[1] Yet it is hard to call it anything else when he and other dispensationalists jump from one Bible verse to another to piece together their chronology of the Rapture. They use the image of buried treasure, claiming that God has hidden individual Rapture verses here and there in the Bible, similar to burying a treasure. But if the doctrine of the Rapture is so central to Christians' future, why did God bury the treasure for 1,800 years? Why do we have to piece it together only to find it now?

As I have argued, the answer is that the Rapture and the dispensationalist chronology is a fabrication. The dispensationalist story creates a comprehensive, overarching narrative that appeals to people who are seeking clear-cut answers. But the dispensationalist system's supposed clear-cut answers rely on a highly selective biblical literalism, as well as insertion of nonexistent two-thousand-year gaps and dubious re-definitions of key terms. The system is not true to a literal reading of the Bible, as they claim. Nor is their system true to the Bible's wonderful richness and complexity. The dispensationalist system narrows the Bible's message.

The following discussions address in greater depth the three principal biblical passages people ask me about most often, which are key to the dispensationalists' Rapture script (see discussion in chapters 2 and 3): First Thessalonians 4:13–18, Matthew 24:40–41, and John 14:1–2. Rather than trying to harmonize these and other passages into an overarching system, it is important to examine each passage in its own historical and theological context. Each of these three early Christian documents was written to address specific concerns in different first-century communities. Paul's letter to the Thessalonians, for example, addresses different questions and emphasizes different aspects of our relationship with Jesus from the Gospels of Matthew or John. That very diversity is the Bible's true treasure. It gives us a richness and depth of relationship with God that far exceeds all of our attempts to systematize it.

1 THESSALONIANS 4:13–18

But we do not want you to be uninformed, brothers and sisters, about those who have died, so that you may not grieve as others do who have no hope. For since we believe that Jesus died and rose again, even so, through Jesus, God will bring with him those who have died. For this we declare to you by the word of the Lord, that we who are alive, who are left until the coming of the Lord, will by no means precede those who have died. For the Lord himself, with a cry of command, with the archangel's call and with the sound of God's trumpet, will descend from heaven, and the dead in Christ will rise first. Then we who are alive, who are left, will be caught up in the clouds together with them to meet the Lord in the air; and so we will be with the Lord forever. Therefore encourage one another with these words. (New Revised Standard Version)

The apostle Paul's first letter to the Thessalonians is the favorite Rapture proof-text for dispensationalists. A closer look at this passage in the overall context of the letter shows that it is not about Rapture, however, but about resurrection from the dead at Christ's second coming. The Thessalonians apparently feared that some family members who had already died before Christ's return would be left behind in their graves when he returned—and they were grieving that separation. Paul wrote to the church in Thessalonika to reassure them that those who have died will also be raised to meet Christ, "and so we shall always be with the Lord." He wrote the letter in order to give comfort and encouragement, using the assurance of Jesus' resurrection from the dead to give assurance of resurrection also for us.

What this letter is emphasizing is not that some will be left behind, but rather that we will all be *together* with our loved ones in our resurrection life. No believer, whether dead or alive, will be separated from Christ or from the community of their loved ones when the Lord comes again. Paul is saying the very opposite of what Rapture proponents claim when they use him to support their terrifying left-behind notion that some people will be taken while others are left. Paul's pastoral concern here is to comfort people by showing that we will all be together in Christ when he comes again. We will not be separated from Christ or from one another.

Rapture proponents use the details of these verses to argue that Christ snatches born-again Christians off the earth to meet him in the air, and then that Christ turns around and takes people back to heaven for seven years. But take a closer look and you see that there is no indication that the Lord switches directions—much less any mention of seven years in heaven. The passage proclaims that Christ will "descend *from* heaven" (1 Thess 4:16)—that is, he is coming down from heaven to earth. There is no reason to think that Jesus will change directions and turn around to go back to heaven after Christians meet him in the air. What the passage is describing is Jesus' second coming to earth, and the resurrection from the dead that will happen when he returns.

Paul's description of "meeting" the Lord in the air employs a very specific Greek word for greeting a visiting dignitary in ancient times: *apantesis*, a practice by which people went outside the city to greet the dignitary and then accompanied him into their city. The same word is used in Matthew 25:6 to describe the bridesmaids who go out to "meet" the bridegroom and then accompany him into the feast, and also in Acts 28:15 to describe the Romans who go out to "meet" Paul as he arrives in their city. We can look at these other usages to see more specifically what Paul means by the term "meet" the Lord.

The key factor with the normal usage of the Greek verb "meet" is this: In no case does the arriving dignitary change directions and go back where he came from after people come to meet him; rather, he continues with them into their house or city. In Matthew, for example, the bridegroom's arrival is greeted with a shout: "Look! Here is the bridegroom. Come out to meet him." But the bridegroom does not then kidnap the bridesmaids and take them away with him after they go out to meet him! Rather, the bridegroom goes with the bridesmaids into the house from where they came, where everyone is waiting for him. Matthew makes this clear: "The bridegroom came, and those who were with him went into the wedding banquet; and the door was shut" (Matt 25:10).

Similarly in Acts 28, the Christians from Rome go out to meet Paul while he is still outside their city gates, because they are so eager to welcome him. "The believers from there, when they heard of us, came as far as the Forum of Apius and Three Taverns to meet us," Acts records. Paul does not then switch directions and take the Christians away from their city after they go out to "meet" him. Rather, Paul accompanies them back where they came from—into their city.

Paul's use of the same word "meet" in First Thessalonians would suggest that Paul is proclaiming a similar "meeting," where both those who are alive and those who are dead go up to "meet" Christ in the air on his way back to earth, and then they accompany him the rest of the way back to earth as he "descends." The central message of this passage is resurrection of the dead. The image of meeting the Lord in the air underscores that every Christian— whether dead or alive—will be resurrected together to greet Jesus when he returns to earth.

Paul does not ever return to this image of meeting Christ in the air in any of his other letters, so we cannot know with any greater detail what he meant. In all his other writings what Paul emphasizes is simply the good news of resurrection from the dead.

MATTHEW 24:39-42 (SEE ALSO LUKE 17:34-35)

The flood came and swept them all away; so too will be the coming of the Son of Man. Two men will be in the field; one will be taken and the other left. Two women will be grinding meal together; one will be taken and one will be left. Keep awake, therefore, for you do not know on what day your Lord is coming.

Only by combining this passage together with First Thessalonians 4 can dispensationalists begin to piece together their notion of "left behind"—their scenario in which some Christians will be taken up suddenly to meet Christ and go back to heaven with him for seven years, while others will be left behind on earth. But here's the problem with their use of this passage from Matthew: Dispensationalists make the leap of assuming that the person "taken" in this passage is a born-again Christian who is taken up to heaven, while the person "left" is an unbeliever who is left behind for judgment. This is a huge leap, since Jesus himself never specifies whether Christians should desire to be taken or to be left! In the overall context of Matthew's Gospel, both the verbs "taken" and "left" (Greek *paralambano* and *aphiemi*) can be either positive or negative.

In the verses immediately preceding this passage, Jesus says that his coming will be like the flood at the time of Noah, when people were "swept away" in judgment. If being "taken" is analogous to being "swept away" in the flood, then it is not a positive fate. That is the argument of New Testament scholar and Anglican bishop N. T. Wright:

> It should be noted that being "taken" in this context means being taken in *judgment*. There is no hint here of a "rapture," a sudden "supernatural" event that would remove individuals from *terra firma* . . . It is a matter, rather, of secret police coming in the night, or of enemies sweeping through a village or city and seizing all they can. (N.T. Wright, *Jesus and the Victory of God*, vol. 1 of *Christian Origins and the Question of God* [London: SPCK; Minneapolis: Fortress, 1996], 366)

If Wright is correct, this means that being "left behind" is actually the desired fate for Christians, whereas being "taken" would mean being carried off by forces of judgment like a death squad. For people living under severe Roman occupation, being taken away in such a way by secret police would probably be a constant fear. B. Brent

McGuire, a Lutheran critic from the conservative Missouri Synod, suggests that the *Left Behind* books have it "entirely backward." McGuire, like Wright, points out that when analyzed in the overall context of the gospel, the word "taken" means being taken away for *judgment*, as in the story of Jesus' being "taken" prisoner by soldiers in Matthew 27:27.[2] "Taken" is not an image for salvation.

The fact is, Matthew's Gospel is not clear on whether "taken" or "left" is the desired fate—whether being "taken" is analogous to Noah rescuing people by taking them into the ark to save them, as dispensationalists argue, or whether being "taken" rather means taken away for judgment, as Wright argues. Similar ambiguity surrounds the word "left." Is being "left" the negative fate the dispensationalists assume, or does it rather have a positive sense, as when Satan "left" Jesus in Matthew 4:11? Matthew seems to be deliberately ambiguous—perhaps because our focus is not supposed to be on worrying about being taken or on being left, but rather on the urgent necessity of readiness for Jesus' return at any moment!

Whatever the desired fate, Jesus' description of people being "taken" or "left" in this passage certainly does not describe a "Rapture" or an event separate from the last judgment, but is rather part of that judgment. Christ's return is a single event in Matthew, with no evidence that it is separated into two events. There is no "Rapture" to heaven followed by seven years of tribulation, followed by another return of Jesus for judgment.

Indeed, in the Gospel of Matthew, Jesus cautions most strongly that we are not supposed to try to figure out the details of the chronology of the end times. Just two verses before our text, right before the reference to Noah and the flood, Jesus tells his followers, "About that day and hour no one knows, neither the angels of heaven nor the Son, but only the Father" (Matt 24:36). Jesus does not intend for us to piece together Bible verses to construct a detailed timetable that even he himself does not know.

We are, however, to be urgent in our waiting. That urgency is the focus of the entire Olivet Discourse of Matthew 24–25. This urgency is highlighted by the four parables that Jesus tells to illustrate his message.

THE SO-CALLED OLIVET DISCOURSE, MATTHEW 24–25

The Matthew passage about people who are taken and left is part of what dispensationalists call the Olivet Discourse, one of Jesus' five long speeches in the Gospel of Matthew. LaHaye calls the Olivet Discourse the "prophetic clothesline on which every other Bible prophecy ought to be hung."[3] With their view that Jesus' prophetic reference to the blooming of the fig tree was fulfilled with the founding of Israel, they think that chapters 24 and 25 of Matthew predict a sequence of other events that were set in motion in 1948 and are accelerating toward a cataclysmic completion in our lifetime.

But as I have argued, prophecy does not mean prediction. Jesus did not intend his prophetic Olivet Discourse to give a play-by-play of predictions that would eventually culminate in a sequence of events thousands of years off into the future, after the United Nations granted statehood to Israel. Rather, Jesus' purpose is to give *exhortation* to his followers to "keep awake" and remain faithful. Urgency and readiness are the message of this important speech. Disciples of Jesus in every generation are to obey his commandments in readiness for his return, whenever it happens. Jesus is not telling us to figure out the detailed sequence of when or how that return will happen.

Most scholars date Matthew's Gospel to around the year 90 A.D., less than one generation after the destruction of Jerusalem by the

Romans. Thus, the immediate context of the destructions described in the Olivet Discourse for the first readers of the gospel was the trauma of the devastating war and destruction that they had just experienced. We should not look two thousand years later for future fulfillment of specific details of Matthew's Olivet Discourse. Rather, Matthew's first readers would have recognized many allusions to events that had just happened, in the war that they had survived. The Jewish Temple had been desecrated and burned; wars and rumors of wars had swirled all around; many people had been "taken" away as captives, to be enslaved or killed. It certainly felt like earth's last days for those who survived the trauma.

The focus of Jesus' Olivet Discourse for Matthew's first readers, and for us, is not prediction but rather *ethics*—as seen by the four vivid parables Jesus tells to underscore this discourse. The four parables or stories all illustrate the importance of readiness and staying awake, of faithfully stewarding what is entrusted to us until Jesus comes again. We do not know when Jesus is returning again. That is why we must live our lives at every moment as Jesus taught us. The message to Matthew's original readers was the same as the message today: Whatever traumas befall us, we are to be urgent in loving our neighbor, urgent in caring for the world that God created, urgent in feeding the hungry and visiting prisoners, urgent in living faithfully as Christ commanded us to live.

In the first parable (Matt 24:45–51) immediately following the saying about the one who is taken while the other is left, Jesus casts his followers in the role of servants whose master has temporarily gone away. The servant's job is to care for the household in the master's absence, to give food to each inhabitant at the proper time. We are that servant, Jesus tells us! The message is that we must love and care for one another and for the household of God's whole world—so that we will be "the servant whom his master will find at work when he arrives" (Matt 24:46). If we fall asleep while Jesus is away, or if we are like the wicked slave who says to himself, "'My master is delayed,' and he begins to beat his fellow slaves, and eats and drinks with drunkards, the master of that slave will come on a day when he does not expect him and at an hour he does not know. He will cut him in pieces and put him with the hypocrites where there will be weeping and gnashing of teeth," the parable warns.

Similarly, the threat of the severe consequences that will result for those who fail to care for people while Jesus is away is also the message of the fourth parable, the story of the judgment of the sheep and the goats (Matt 25:31–46). Lindsey applies this parable only to those left behind after the Rapture, and then only to the few who survive the seven-year tribulation. For Lindsey, the predictive message of the parable is that "tribulation survivors" will be judged on the basis of how they welcomed a specific group—the 144,000 Jewish evangelists.[4] But such a bizarre interpretation totally misses the ethical urgency of the parable for all of us. There is no evidence that "one of the least of these my brothers and sisters" in Matthew 25:40 refers to Revelation's 144,000. Rather, the parable calls all of us to give an account to God on the basis of how we treat our neighbors who are in need. The "goats" are people who fail to welcome the stranger, who fail to give food to the hungry or clothe the naked or visit the prisoners. Jesus says that if we fail to do such deeds for "one of the least of these"—that is, for our neighbor in need—then we have failed to do these things for Jesus himself, since Jesus is present in every stranger who asks for a cup of water from us.

The message of the third parable (Matt 25:14–30) is similar to the first, that the master of the household will return, and he will ask us to give an account for how we have cared for God's resources in the household of the world. Hoarding our resources or failing to multiply our talents will result in judgment.

Living together as faithful servants ready for Jesus' return—not speculating about the end-times—is the central ethical urgency of all these parables and of Matthew's entire Olivet Discourse. Abusing people or abusing the household of God's creation will carry severe consequences, Jesus says. This is a very different message from the dispensationalists' escapist and nonethical reading of this discourse.

Dispensationalists view the Olivet Discourse as predictive—literal predictions of a linear sequence of world events that must happen in our day in order for Jesus to return. But the most glaring problem with such a literalist approach is Matthew 24:34, where Jesus says: "Truly I tell you, this generation will not pass away until all these things have taken place." Two thousand years have now passed since Jesus spoke these words, and the people he addressed as "this generation" have long since passed away—yet the specific events of which he spoke did not literally happen as exactly as dispensationalists say they must. The dispensationalist solution is to arbitrarily redefine Jesus' term "this generation" so that "this generation" means not Jesus' original audience, but a generation of people two thousand years later, the generation that began with Israel's founding as a state in 1948, or with Israel's taking of the West Bank and East Jerusalem in 1967. Lindsey calls those of us living today "the generation of the fig tree," referring to his interpretation of the founding of Israel as the fig tree putting forth its buds in Matthew 24:32. Such a move has no literal basis in the Bible itself, however, nor is it true to their "plain sense" rule of interpretation. It is an example of their highly selective literalism—with no biblical evidence to support this redefinition of "this generation."

JOHN 14:1-2

In my Father's house are many dwellings. If it were not so, would I
have told you that I go to prepare a place for you?

Rapture proponents like to point to Jesus' farewell words in John
14:1–2 as the "first teaching about Rapture in the Bible."[5] They
argue that Jesus' statement that he is going away to "prepare a
place for you" means that he is going away to heaven to get a place
ready for those who will be Raptured. "In my father's house are
many dwellings," Jesus says, using a Greek word that means "rest-
ing place" or "way station": *mone*, from the verb "abide" or "remain."
But the problem is that Jesus does not specify where the Father's
house is located. Is it in heaven, as Rapture proponents argue? Not
necessarily, or at least not exclusively in the Gospel of John,
because later in the same chapter Jesus says that he and the Father
will come and make their "dwelling"—using the very same word—
in the believing person: "We will come and make our dwelling
[*mone*] with that one" (John 14:23). Here the image surely means
God's mystical indwelling in the believer. The Gospel of John is the
most mystical of all our gospels, and it is very hard to pin down
locations or chronologies in this Gospel.

Robert Gundry, a conservative evangelical scholar, cautions
against assuming that Jesus' "many dwellings" or "many mansions"
are rooms up in heaven. For Gundry, the crucial clue is that Jesus
never promises that, upon his return, Jesus will take the disciples
away to the "dwellings" or "mansions" in the Father's house, as one
would expect in the dispensationalists' literalist scenario. Rather,
what Jesus promised to the disciples is that "Where I am, you will
be also." Gundry views the key to chapter 14 as the two parallel
occurrences of *mone*—verses 2 and 23. These verses provide a

"reciprocal relationship: [A]s believers have abiding-places in Christ, so Jesus and the Father have an abiding-place in each believer."[6]

In Gundry's view the "father's house" in John's gospel is not so much heaven as God's household or family on earth. Indeed, the word "house" is probably better translated as "household" both here and in John 4:53 and 8:35. In a strong and mystical sense, John wants to underscore that we are *already* in some sense living in the mystical "dwelling places" in the Father's household that Jesus says he has prepared for us. The passage is about "not mansions in the sky, but spiritual positions in Christ."[7] Jesus is the vine and we are the branches who "dwell" or "abide" in him already, to use the similar mystical imagery that is found in John 15. It is not a matter of being taken away from planet earth, up to the Father's house in heaven. The dwelling Jesus is preparing for us is something quite different.

In the Gospel of John, imagery of ascending and descending has a rich, double meaning that makes a strictly "heavenist" interpretation impossible. Far more important than going up to heaven in John's gospel is the in-ness and one-ness Jesus wants us to experience already with God. The gospel's focus is on the rich relationship of mutual indwelling and eternal life that is already ours. To know God is to have eternal life—"this is eternal life," Jesus says in his great farewell prayer (John 17:3).

Never would John's Gospel say that Jesus and God are now up in heaven, waiting until the end-times in order to come back to earth and take us away to heaven in the Rapture and then in the Glorious Appearing. God dwells with us now, on earth, in mystical communion through the Spirit or Paraclete, in John's Gospel. To impose the linear timeline of Rapture followed by tribulation and then an earthly return imports a chronology that is totally foreign to the Gospel of John.

WRESTLING WITH THE BIBLE:
A PROPHETIC CLOTHESLINE OR A BLESSING?

The Bible is difficult to understand, and apocalyptic passages such as the book of Revelation and Matthew 24–25 are some of the hardest. The temptation is to make up a system to give answers— to create a "prophetic clothesline" and then hang biblical passages on it. But the Bible gives us neither a clothesline nor a timeline nor a system—it gives us a relationship with God! To read the Bible's hardest passages is like wrestling with God, much like Jacob who wrestled through the night at the river Jabbok.[8] You grapple to make sense of the words, you hold on, you struggle for clarity, you seek to wrest answers for all your questions. What God gives you instead of a system of answers is a blessing, a new name—a living relationship. You are forever changed by the encounter. You have seen the face of God.

We could examine each of the many other biblical passages that dispensationalists love to cite. The fact is that not one single biblical passage lays out the dispensationalists' overarching chronology of Rapture followed by seven years of tribulation followed by Jesus' return to earth. They have to piece this grand narrative together like stringing clothes on a clothesline. There is no two-stage return of Christ in the Bible, no escapist Rapture from earth for born-again Christians.

Jesus will return—once. Until then, we are always with Jesus and he is with us—Emmanuel. Our life is held in God's time. And we are called to live in wakefulness, to pray as the final verses of Revelation do, "Amen, come Lord Jesus."

NOTES

CHAPTER 1: THE DESTRUCTIVE RHETORIC OF RAPTURE

1. John Hagee, *From Daniel to Doomsday: The Countdown Has Begun* (Nashville, Tenn.: Thomas Nelson, 1999), 117.

2. Hal Lindsey, *The Rapture: Truth or Consequences* (NY: Bantam Books, 1983) 210.

3. Ibid., 121.

4. Jim Bakker, *Prosperity and the Coming Apocalypse* (Nashville, Tenn.: Thomas Nelson, 1998).

5. Tim LaHaye, *Revelation Illustrated and Made Plain*, rev. ed. (Grand Rapids, Mich.: Zondervan, 1973), 307.

6. Romans 8:19–23.

7. "Hannity and Colmes," June 20, 2001; quoted in "The Wisdom of Ann Coulter," the *Washington Monthly*, October 2001, www.washingtonmonthly.com/features/2001/0111.coulterwisdom.html.

8. C. S. Lewis, *The Last Battle* (New York: Macmillan, 1956), 181, emphasis is the author's.

9. Genesis 8:21.

10. From *Narrative of Sojourner Truth: A Bondswoman of Olden Time, With a History of Her Labors and Correspondence Drawn from Her "Book of Life,"* The Schomburg Library of Nineteenth-Century Black Women Writers (NY: Oxford University Press, 1991), 168.

11. See 2 Corinthians 1:20, "For the Son of God, Jesus Christ, whom we proclaimed among you . . . was not 'Yes and No,' but in him it is always 'Yes.' For in him every one of God's promises is a 'Yes.'"

12. Gerard Manley Hopkins, "God's Grandeur," in John F. Thornton and Susan B. Varenne, eds., *Mortal Beauty, God's Grace: Major Poems and Spiritual Writings of Gerard Manley Hopkins* (NY: Random House, 2003), 21.

13. Tim LaHaye and Jerry Jenkins, *The Remnant: On the Brink of Armageddon*, vol. 10 of *Left Behind* series (Wheaton, Ill.: Tyndale House Publishers, 2003), 252, 277.

14. Paul Boyer, *When Time Shall Be No More: Prophecy Belief in American Culture* (Cambridge, Mass: Harvard University Press, 1990), 97. Premillennialists interpret Revelation 20 to claim that Christ will have a literal, 1,000-year reign on earth based in Jerusalem. No other New Testament passage makes reference to any such reign, nor is it mentioned in any of the early church's creeds.

15. Ibid., 97; quoting nineteenth-century preacher Nathaniel West, *Premillennial Essays.*

16. Ibid., 95.

17. Randall Balmer and Michael Maudlin, "The Left Behind Books," slate.com Book Club, June 20, 2002, 2; http://slate.msn.com/id/2000179.

18. LaHaye and Jenkins, *The Remnant*, 94.

19. Ibid., 180.

20. Ibid., 45–46.

21. Pablo Richard, *Apocalypse: A People's Commentary on the Book of Revelation* (Maryknoll, NY: Orbis, 1995).

22. *Letters of Pliny the Younger* 10.96; trans. Eugene Boring, *Revelation* (Interpretation Commentaries; Louisville, Kent.: John Knox Press, 1989) 14–15.

CHAPTER 2: THE INVENTION OF THE RAPTURE

1. Tim LaHaye and Jerry Jenkins, *Left Behind: A Novel of Earth's Last Day*, vol. 1 of *Left Behind* series (Wheaton, Ill.: Tyndale House Publishers, 1996), 126.

2. Dave MacPherson, *The Rapture Plot,* 2d ed. (Simpsonville, S.C.: Millennium III Publishers, 2000).

3. Boyer, *When Time Shall Be No More*, 248 and 346 n. 23. Tim LaHaye disputes the attribution of the Raptured to Margaret MacDonald, arguing that Macdonald saw a vision of a *post*-tribulation Rapture, not a pre-tribulation Rapture. See LaHaye, *The Rapture: Who Will Face the Tribulation?* (Eugene, Ore.: Harvest House Publishers, 2002), 173–187.

4. Dave MacPherson, "The End is Not Near," *The Door Magazine*, September/October 2001, 13.

5. Lindsey, *The Rapture: Truth or Consequences*, 57.

6. Ibid., 3–4.

7. LaHaye, *The Rapture: Who Will Face the Tribulation?*, 43.

8. "Plain sense" is what Hal Lindsey calls his "golden rule of interpretation": "When the plain sense of Scripture makes common sense, seek no other sense; therefore, take every word at its primary, ordinary, usual, literal meaning unless the facts of the immediate context, studied in the light of related passages and axiomatic and fundamental truths, indicate clearly otherwise." *The Late Great Planet Earth*, 40.

9. Hagee, *From Daniel to Doomsday*, 41.

10. Tim LaHaye with Steve Halliday, *The Merciful God of Prophecy: His Loving Plan for You in the End Times* (NY: Warner Books, 2002), 143; emphasis is the author's.

11. Hagee, *From Daniel to Doomsday*, 25.

12. Martin Marty, "Peddlers of the Ultimate Axis of Evil," *Context*, February 15, 2003, 6.

13. *Charting the End Times* is the title of one of LaHaye's other books (Wheaton, Ill.: Tyndale House Publishers, 2002).

14. Lindsey, *The Rapture: Truth or Consequences*, 7.

15. LaHaye, *The Merciful God of Prophecy*, 155.

16. LaHaye and Jenkins, *Left Behind*, 209.

17. Ibid., 210.

18. LaHaye, *The Rapture: Who Will Face the Tribulation?* 41.

19. The Thessalonians apparently feared that some family members who had died would be left behind in their graves when Christ returns. Paul writes to reassure them that those who have died will also be raised to meet Christ, "and so we shall always be with the Lord." The image of meeting the Lord in the air underscores that all will be resurrected to greet Jesus' return to earth. Since the passage first of all proclaims that Christ "descends" (1 Thess 4:16), there is no reason to assume that Jesus will change directions and turn around to go back to heaven once Christians meet him in the air. (See Epilogue)

20. For the puzzle image see LaHaye, *The Rapture: Who Will Face the Tribulation?*, 135.

21. LaHaye, *The Merciful God of Prophecy*, 161.

22. Lindsey, *The Rapture: Truth or Consequences*, 37.

23. Catholic Conference of Illinois Bishops' Statement on *Left Behind* books and videos, June 24, 2003. For full text see www.zenit.org.

24. LaHaye, *The Merciful God of Prophecy*, 139.

25. There is no indication that "he" in Daniel 9:27 refers to the Antichrist as the one making a convenant for one week. The previous verse, in fact, suggests that "he" refers to "the anointed one" or Messiah—a problem dispensationalists never address.

26. http://www.leftbehind.com, "Frequently Asked Questions."

27. LaHaye and Jenkins, *Left Behind,* 312.

28. Gary DeMar, *End Times Fiction: A Biblical Consideration of the Left Behind Theology* (Nashville, Tenn.: Thomas Nelson, 2001), 44.

29. Ibid., 32.

30. Craig Hill, *In God's Time: The Bible and The Future* (Grand Rapids, Mich.: Eerdmans, 2002), 207.

31. Pat Robertson, *The End of the Age* (Dallas, Tex.: Word Books, 1995).

32. Wolf Blitzer, *Jerusalem Post,* Oct. 28, 1983; quoted in Landau, "The President and the Bible: What Do the Prophets Say to Our Time?" *Christianity and Crisis,* Dec. 12, 1983, 474.

33. Boyer, *When Time Shall Be No More,* 142.

34. Landau, "The President and the Bible," 475.

CHAPTER 3: THE RAPTURE'S SCRIPT FOR THE MIDDLE EAST

1. Revelation 21–22.

2. Ibid., 55–56.

3. See also Tim LaHaye and Jerry Jenkins, *Are We Living in the Endtimes?* (Wheaton, Ill.: Tyndale House Publishers, 1999), 128–129.

4. Randall Price, *The Coming Last Days Temple* (Eugene, Ore.: Harvest House, 1999), 271–273.

5. Revelation 11:19; 15:5.

6. Lindsey, *The Late Great Planet Earth,* 56.

7. Grace Halsell, *Forcing God's Hand: Why Millions Pray for a Quick Rapture— And Destruction of Planet Earth* (Beltsville, MD: Amana Publications, 1999).

8. Gershom Gorenberg, *The End of Days: Fundamentalism and the Struggle for the Temple Mount* (NY: Oxford University Press, 2000).

9. Ibid., 11.

10. "Zion's Christian Soldiers," *Sixty Minutes,* October 6, 2002; http://cbsnews.com/stories/2002/10/03/60minutes/main524268.html.

11. Gorenberg, *The End of Days,* 240.

12. Naim Stifan Ateek, *Justice and Only Justice: A Palestinian Theology of Liberation* (Maryknoll, NY: Orbis Books, 1989), 10.

13. See Charles M. Sennott, *The Body and The Blood: The Middle East's Vanishing Christians and the Possibility for Peace* (New York: Public Affairs, 2001), 33.

14. Halsell, *Forcing God's Hand,* 59.

15. Timothy Weber, "How Evangelicals Became Israel's Best Friend," *Christianity Today* 42 (1998). See also Gary Burge, *Whose Land? Whose Promise? What*

Christians Are Not Being Told About Israel and the Palestinians (Cleveland, Ohio: Pilgrim Press, 2003).

16. Richard Mouw, "How to Bless Israel," Beliefnet, http://www.beliefnet.org/story/106/story_10688_2.html, accessed May 31, 2002.

17. For full text of the letter and list of signatories, see the Churches for Middle East Peace Web site, http://www.cmep.org/alerts/2002Jul12-1.htm.

18. David Dolen, *Israel in Crisis: What Lies Ahead?* (Grand Rapids, Mich.: Fleming H. Revell Co., 2001).

19. So Danielle Haas, "U.S. Christians Find Cause to Aid Israel: Evangelicals Financing Immigrants, Settlements," *San Francisco Chronicle*, July 10, 2002.

20. "The transfer by the Occupying Power of parts of its own civilian population into the territory it occupies, or the deportation or transfer of all or parts of the population of the occupied territory within or outside this territory" is to be regarded as a "grave breach" of the Geneva Convention Protocol of 12 August 1949 relating to the Protection of Victims of International Armed Conflicts (Protocol 1) and reiterated in 1977 by the United Nations High Commissioner for Human Rights; http://www.unhchr.ch/html/menu3/b/93.htm.

21. For details on the poll see the Web site of the International Crisis Group, http://www.intl-crisisgroup.org/home/index.cfm?id=2384&1=1.

22. For the full text of the Nusseibeh/Ayalon petition, see http://www.cmep.org/documents/peoplesvoice.htm. See also the official Web site, http://www.mifkad.org.il/eng.

23. For more information go to http://www.cfoic.com.

24. BBC Radio, "Analysis: America's New Christian Zionists," May 7, 2002.

25. Nancy Gibbs, "Apocalypse Now," *Time*, July 1, 2002, 42.

26. CNBC "Hardball," May 1, 2002; for transcript, see http://www.counterpunch.org/armey0502.html.

27. See "Declaration of the Evangelical Lutheran Church in American to the Jewish Community," April 18, 1994: "In the spirit of truth-telling, we . . . must with pain acknowledge also Luther's anti-Judaic diatribes and the violent recommendations of his later writings against the Jews. As did many of Luther's own companions in the sixteenth century, we reject this violent invective, and yet more do we express our deep and abiding sorrow over its tragic effects on subsequent generations . . . We particularly deplore the appropriation of Luther's words by modern anti-Semites for teaching of hatred toward Judaism." http://www.elca.org/ea.

28. "Zion's Christian Soldiers," *Sixty Minutes*, Oct. 6, 2002.

29. Amy Johnson Frykholm, *Rapture Culture: Left Behind in Evangelical America* (NY: Oxford University Press, forthcoming 2004).

30. Munib Younan, *Witnessing for Peace in Jerusalem and the World* (Minneapolis, Minn.: Fortress Press, 2003).

31. See Yehezkel Landau, "Blessing Both Jew and Palestinian: A Religious Zionist View," *The Christian Century*, December 20-27, 1989; "Healing the Holy Land: Interreligious Peacebuilding in Israel/Palestine" (Washington, DC: U.S. Institute of Peace, 2003); www.usip.org/pubs/peaceworks/pwks51. pdf.

32. For Dalia's story and information about Open House see http:// www.friendsofopenhouse.org.

CHAPTER 4: PROPHECY AND APOCALYPSE

1. "The Revelation Revolution Keeps on Spinning," *Minneapolis Star-Tribune*, April 5, 2003.

2. Martha Himmelfarb, *Tours of Hell: An Apocalyptic Form in Jewish and Christian Literature* (Philadelphia, Penn.: Fortress Press, 1981).

3. Barbara Rossing, *The Choice Between Two Cities: Whore, Bride, and Empire in the Apocalypse* (Harrisburg, Penn.: Trinity Press International, 1999).

4. Landau, "The President and the Bible," 474.

5. Elizabeth Schüssler Fiorenza, *Revelation: Vision of a Just World* (Minneapolis, Minn.: Fortress Press, 1991).

6. Tim LaHaye and Jerry Jenkins, *Soul Harvest: The World Takes Sides*, vol. 4 of *Left Behind* (Wheaton, Ill.: Tyndale House Publishers, 1999), 33.

7. Ibid., 63.

8. http://www.leftbehind.com. "Interpreting the Signs: Current Events Foretold in Scripture . . . And What They Mean" (June/July 2003).

9. LaHaye and Jenkins, *Armageddon*, 350.

10. LaHaye and Jenkins, *Nicolae*, 327.

11. Ibid., 136.

12. Kathleen Norris, Introduction to *Revelation*, Pocket Canon Series (New York: Grove Press, 1999), 11.

13. LaHaye and Jenkins, *Soul Harvest*, 410.

CHAPTER 5: THE JOURNEY BEGINS

1. Clifford Ando, *Imperial Ideology and Provincial Loyalty in the Roman Empire* (Berkeley, Calif.: University of California Press, 2000), 280.

2. *Coins of the Roman Empire in the British Museum*, vol. 2, 47.

3. Bill Jobling, "The Aqaba-Ma'an Archaeological and Epigraphic Survey 1988–90," *Syria* 70 (1993), 244.

4. Revelation 18:13. This is the only outright condemnation of slavery or slave trade in the entire New Testament.

5. Amanda Claridge, *Rome: An Oxford Archaeological Guide* (NY: Oxford University Press, 1999), 118.

6. Steven Friesen, *Imperial Cults and the Apocalypse of John: Reading Revelation in the Ruins* (NY: Oxford University Press, 2001).

7. Ward Ewing, *The Power of the Lamb: Revelation's Theology of Liberation for You* (Cambridge, Mass.: Cowley Press, 1990), 19.

CHAPTER 6: LAMB POWER

1. David Barr, *Tales of the End: A Narrative Commentary on the Book of Revelation* (Santa Rosa, Calif.: Polebridge Press, 1998), 3.

2. David Barr, "Towards an Ethical Reading of the Apocalypse," *Society of Biblical Literature 1997 Seminar Papers* (Atlanta, GA: Scholars Press, 1997), 361.

3. 2 Esdras 11–12.

4. Daniel Erlander, personal communication with the author.

5. Testament of Joseph 19.8 does speak of a "spotless lamb," who was born of a virgin and "conquered," but this is probably a later Christian interpolation in this Jewish apocalypse. See H. C. Kee, "Testaments of the Twelve Patriarchs: A New Translation and Introduction," in James H. Charlesworth, ed., *The Old Testament Pseudepigrapha: Apocalyptic Literature and Testaments*, vol. 2 (NY: Doubleday, 1983), 824. Similarly, David Aune argues that "the Messiah is never symbolized as a lamb in Judaism" and that Revelation's lamb is original to this author. *Revelation 1–5*, Word Biblical Commentary 52a (Dallas, Tex.: Word Books, 1997), 353.

6. Memories of door-knocking Jehovah's Witnesses may frighten us away from passages such as Revelation 14:1–4 that seem to specify a specific number for those saved as 144,000 (see also Rev 7:4). But the number 144,000 is not meant to be literal. It is rather a very large number, symbolic of a multiple of the twelve tribes of Israel and the twelve apostles, a "multitude that no one can count" (Rev 7:9). A strictly literal reading of the whole passage is impossible, since it would necessitate that Jesus be a sheep and also that his followers consist of only 144,000 male virgins—a fact that few married male literalists want to allow! But selective literalism has no justification. If the 144,000 followers are not literally male virgins, and if Jesus is not literally a sheep, then it makes no sense to insist on reading other aspects of this scene literally. We also must reject the

interpretation of dispensationalists who insist that the 144,000 consist exclusively of (male) Jewish converts to Christianity after the rapture, whose role is to populate the millennial kingdom.

7. Richard, *Apocalypse: A People's Commentary*, 117.

8. Christine LeMoignan, *Following the Lamb: A Reading of Revelation for the New Millenium* (London: SCM Press, 2000).

9. Ewing, *The Power of the Lamb*, 198.

10. Ibid., 109; the remarks about September 11 were given in a lecture at the Anglican Association of Biblical Scholars in Denver, Colorado, November 2001.

CHAPTER 7: NONVIOLENCE

1. LaHaye and Jenkins, *Soul Harvest*, 414.

2. John Howard Yoder, *The Politics of Jesus* (Grand Rapids, Mich.: Eerdmans, 1972); see especially chapter 12, "The War of the Lamb."

3. Lee Griffith, *The War on Terrorism and the Terror of God* (Grand Rapids, Mich.: Eerdmans, 2002), 205. For nonviolence in Revelation see also Nelson Kraybill, *Imperial Cult and Commerce in John's Apocalypse*, JSNT Sup 132 (Sheffield, England: Sheffield Academic Press, 1996); Walter Wink, *Engaging the Powers: Discernment and Resistance in a World of Domination*, The Powers vol. 3 (Minneapolis, Minn.: Fortress Press, 1992); Steven Friesen, *Imperial Cults*.

4. Richard, *Apocalypse: A People's Commentary*, 33 and 74.

5. Lindsey, *The Late Great Planet Earth*, 173–174.

6. David Barr, "Towards an Ethical Reading of the Apocalypse," 362.

CHAPTER 8: THE EXODUS STORY IN REVELATION

1. Richard, *Apocalypse: A People's Commentary*, 86.

2. Elisabeth Schüssler Fiorenza, *Revelation: Vision of a Just World*, 72.

3. Ibid., 73.

4. For the full argument that "woe" is not a good translation for the Greek word *ouai* in Revelation, see Barbara Rossing, "Alas for the Earth! Lament and Resistance in Revelation 12," in Norman Habel and Shirley Wurst, eds., *The Earth Story in the New Testament* (Sheffield, England: Sheffield Academic Press, 2002).

5. Schüssler Fiorenza, *Revelation: Vision of a Just World*, 72.

6. See the critique of Tina Pippin, *Death and Desire: The Rhetoric of Gender in the Apocalypse of John* (Louisville, Ken.: Westminster, 1992).

CHAPTER 9: HIJACKING THE LAMB

1. John Hagee, *From Daniel to Doomsday*, 239.

2. Ibid., 239.

3. Lindsey, *The Late Great Planet Earth*, 169. The "main event" is the chapter title.

4. Tim LaHaye and Jerry Jenkins, *Are We Living in the End Times?* (Wheaton, Ill.: Tyndale House Publishers, 1999), 228.

5. Hagee, *From Daniel to Doomsday*, 217.

6. Carl McIntire, *Christian Beacon*, June 24, 1965; quoted in Halsell, *Forcing God's Hand*, 36.

7. Chris Hedges, *War Is a Force That Gives Us Meaning* (New York: Public Affairs, 2002), 89.

8. Revelation 18:23.

9. Chris Hedges, interview on *Now with Bill Moyers*, PBS Television, March 7, 2003. http://www.pbs.org/now/transcript/transcript_hedges.html.

CHAPTER 10: RAPTURE IN REVERSE

1. Lindsey, *The Late Great Planet Earth*, 169.

2. Justo Gonzales, *For the Healing of the Nations: The Book of Revelation in an Age of Cultural Conflict* (Maryknoll, NY: Orbis, 1999), 59.

3. Richard, *Apocalypse: A People's Commentary*, 67.

4. C. S. Lewis, *The Last Battle*.

5. "Heavenism" is a term coined by Norman Habel. See his five-volume series *The Earth Bible* (Sheffield, England: Sheffield Academic Press), especially his essay "Introducing the Earth Bible." In *Readings from the Perspective of the Earth*, ed. Norman C. Habel (Sheffield, England: Sheffield Academic Press, 2002), 24–37.

6. "Remaining Awake Through a Great Revolution," March 31, 1968, in James M. Washington, ed., *A Testament of Hope: The Essential Writings and Speeches of Martin Luther King, Jr.* (San Francisco, Calif.: Harper San Francisco, 1986), 277–278.

7. Ezekiel 47.

8. See Barbara Rossing, "River of Life in God's New Jerusalem: An Eschatological Vision for Earth's Future," in Rosemary Radford Ruether and Dieter Hessel, eds., *Christianity and Ecology* (Cambridge, Mass.: Harvard University Press; Center for World Religions, 1999), 205–224.

9. Dieter Georgi, "Die Visionen vom himmlischen Jerusalem in Apk 21 u 22," in Dieter Lührmann and Georg Strecke, eds., *Kirche: Festschrift für Günther Bornkamm* (Tübingen, Germany: Mohr/Siebeck, 1980), 369.

10. John 7:37–39.

11. See Larry Rasmussen, "Trees of Life," in *Earth Community Earth Ethics* (Maryknoll, NY: Orbis, 1994), 195–219.

CHAPTER 11: THE JOURNEY OUTWARD

1. Annie Dillard, *Pilgrim at Tinker Creek* (NY: Perennial, 1988), 33.

2. Ugo Vanni, "Liturgical Dialogue as a Literary Form in Revelation," *New Testament Studies* 37 (1991), 360.

3. Ward Ewing, 176.

4. William Blake, "Milton," in Alfred Kazin, ed., *The Portable Blake* (NY: Viking Portable Library, Penguin, 1946), 412.

5. Dorothee Soelle, *The Silent Cry: Mysticism and Resistance* (Minneapolis, Minn.: Fortress Press, 2001), 293.

6. "The Columbia River Pastoral Letter Project," www.columbiariver.org.

7. William Skylstad, "The Waters of Life," in Brian Doyle, ed., *God is Love: Essays from Portland Magazine* (Minneapolis, Minn.: Augsburg Fortress Publishers, 2003), 82.

8. Kathleen Norris, Introduction to *Revelation*, Pocket Canon Series (NY: Grove Press, 1999), 12.

EPILOGUE

1. Lindsey, *The Late Great Planet Earth*, 119.

2. "Will You Be Left Behind?" *The Lutheran Witness*, March 2001, http://www.lcms.org/cic/lbwitness.htm.

3. LaHaye, *The Merciful God of Prophecy*, 120.

4. Lindsey, *The Rapture: Truth or Consequences*, 172–175.

5. LaHaye, *The Merciful God of Prophecy*, 155.

6. Robert Gundry, "'In my Father's House are Many *Monai*' (John 14:2)," *Zeitschrift für die Neutestamentliche Wissenchaft*, 58 (1969), 68–72.

7. Ibid., 70.

8. Genesis 32:22–32.

ACKNOWLEDGMENTS

Much of this book was first presented as lectures at the Holden Village retreat center and in churches and other settings. Responses from pastors' conferences and synod assemblies, especially the Rocky Mountain Synod of the Evangelical Lutheran Church in America—at the invitation Bishop Allan Bjornberg—helped to shape the book's imagery and argument. Chapter 7 expands on a Bible study presented at the People's Seminary, facilitated by Bob Ekblad. Parts of chapters 4, 10, and 11 reflect material developed for Bible studies on Revelation and the Rapture for the *SELECT* video series, as well as Bible studies for the Lutheran World Federation's tenth assembly study book, *For the Healing of the World*, edited by Karen Bloomquist. An invitation from Fortress Press to write a "New Proclamation" commentary for preachers on the lectionary texts for Easter C (2001) laid the initial groundwork for much of this book.

Elisabeth Schüssler Fiorenza, Helmut Koester, and Allen Callahan at Harvard first guided my interest in the biblical book of Revelation, and I give thanks especially to Elisabeth. Her work on the rhetoric and ethics of Revelation is foundational for scholarship on

Revelation today. I am grateful for the contributions of many colleagues and students at the Lutheran School of Theology at Chicago, and for support of Dean Kadi Billman and President James Kenneth Echols. A 2001 conference on Revelation, organized by David Rhoads and Mark Thomsen of the Chicago Center for Global Ministries, brought together global and multicultural voices including Pablo Richard, Vítor Westhelle, and others, and helped clarify my own thinking on Revelation and the destructive rhetoric of Rapture. I am especially grateful to Amy Johnson Frykholm for sharing the manuscript of her forthcoming book *The Rapture Culture: Left Behind in Evangelical America*, with the image of "scripture coming to life" in the compelling power of a storyline .

A year-long leave in Wenatchee, Washington, during the academic year 2002–2003 was made possible by a generous Christian Faith and Life Sabbatical Grant from the Louisville Institute. A sabbatical grant from Thrivent Financial for Lutherans funded travel and research in the Middle East.

For assistance with the manuscript, thanks goes most of all to Ann Hafften, coordinator for Middle East networking for the Evangelical Lutheran Church in America, to whom this book is dedicated, as well as to Lauren Johnson and Susan Thomas. Pastors Michael and Susan Thomas at Redeemer Lutheran Church provided wonderful hospitality in Jerusalem in December 2002. Yehezkel and Dalia Landau, Pastor Mitri Raheb, Father Naim Ateek, Bishop Munib Younan, Daniel Rossing, the Christian Peacemaker Team, and many others in the Middle East were more than generous. I am grateful to my parents, Dorothy and Tom Rossing, and to my sisters and family for all their encouragement over many long years.

Thanks to friends and colleagues who sent clippings of news articles or made helpful suggestions about the political or cultural impact of the Rapture and Revelation, including Jonathan Frerichs,

Jackie Brolsma, Valarie Ziegler, Dan Erlander, Audrey West, Paul Elbert, Ellen Aitken, Cynthia Kittredge, Liz and Rich Caemmerer of the Grunewald Guild, Mary Schramm and Tom Witt, and other partners in Union Valley, colleagues in the Society of Biblical Literature's "John's Apocalypse and Cultural Contexts Ancient and Modern" section, and many others. I am grateful to the Fellowship of Reconciliation and to Lutheran Peace Fellowship and other peace fellowships for their tireless work for nonviolence in a time of war.

I am grateful to Sarah Warner, my editor at Westview, whose invaluable suggestions and encouragement brought this book to its current form. I am grateful to Jim Levine, my agent at the Levine Greenberg Literary Agency. Thanks goes to Lori Hobkirk at The Book Factory for copyediting and managing the project through its production phase, and to Katherine Shaner for indexing. Kulia the cat—one of God's "dear creatures" as C. S. Lewis calls them—sat with me faithfully through many early morning hours of writing. Thank you to all.

INDEX

DATE DUE

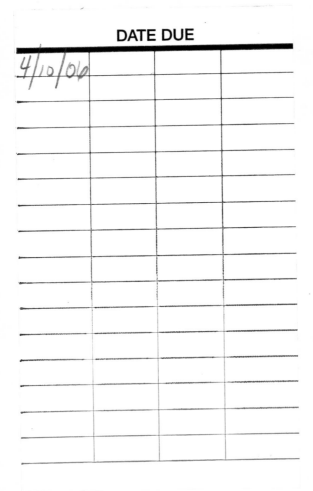

4/10/06